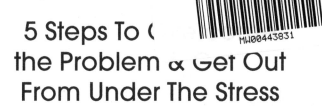

5 Steps To (
the Problem & Get Out
From Under The Stress

Coping Smart.

*To Leyla,
Who thinks outside the box!*

*Love,
Bebe*

Becki Pickett, M.C.P

Published by CapStar Publishing Dallas, TX

 CapStar Publishing

Cover design by Jeremy Glisson

Cover photography by © Rawpixelimages | Dreamstime.com

Author photo by Judith Hill Photography

Print ISBN: 978-1-7367542-7-6
Ebook ISBN: 978-1-7367542-3-8

Table of Contents

Introduction

I know this place where you are right now. You've got a problem.

You were going along just fine. Life was good. Then something changed. Someone broke your heart, or you lost your job, or your child went off track, or a medical report changed everything, or you woke up to a world rocked in ways you didn't see coming.

A problem of any size causes stress. Stress causes confusion. Confusion causes your mind to become fertile ground where doubt, indecision, disappointment, and dissatisfaction grow until your mind fills with distress. That distress chokes your happiness.

You're sure no one can possibly understand exactly what you're going through. They don't really know you, or your screwed up family, or the unbearable grief, or your intolerable workplace, or your miserable relationship, or the disappointment, or the regret, or the unfulfilled dream, or the hard choices, or the feeling of being trapped, or the _____ . Fill in the blank.

I've been there. I've helped others in the same place. I know these feelings.

The problems may have been different than the one you're facing, but they put me in a place of the same emotional distress. You're trying to figure out how you got here, how to get out, and, most urgently, how to cope with the emotions coursing through your body and mind until you find a solution to the problem that works for you.

Problems are as unique to you as your fingerprints. Your family legacy, your personality, your experiences, and your relationships are what make you, you. Your story is your story. No two people experience the same type of problem the same way.

No one gets a pass, and problems happen to everyone throughout a lifetime.

That's not a Debbie Downer message, it's simply a fact. You know that.

Sometimes the problem comes *to* you. Sometimes it comes *from* you. Either way, what matters right now is that you may feel helpless and out of control. These feelings magnify the problem's effect with the stress it is causing.

Maybe the problem that you're facing is a simple aggravation or irritation, sort of like a pebble stuck in your shoe that's got you off your game and out of step. It might be the pressure of something stronger and overwhelming like a boulder of pain that's pinning you down. Or you're feeling something in between.

You're anxious.

You're worried.

You're mad as hell.

You ache in a way you never imagined.

You may be feeling a combination of emotions, and the effect is negatively affecting other parts of your life. You might be unable to name the emotion, but you know it has a hold on you that you can't seem to shake.

Right now, you wish you had an immunity to these feelings, that there was a preventative pill to protect you from them, or a magic mantra to make the problem and the pain go away.

The problem may have been in your life for a long time or recent events brought it on. It could be global or particular to you. Either way you're looking for relief. You've done all the things the experts suggest, but you need more help managing the situation.

You don't need bumper sticker platitudes.

You've collected all the inspirational memes you could ever want.

You've been faithful with your gratitude journaling.

You've made a kick-ass vision board.

You've practiced being mindful and tried meditation.

You've listened to the positivity podcasts.

You've gone barefoot and grounded with nature.

You reminded yourself to breathe deeply rather than involuntarily.

Now, all of those may have begun to feel like more burden on top of the pile. You have or are now experiencing the burn-out that often follows the boost of relief when it fades.

The problem remains.

The stress mounts. It may even morph. It can manifest in all kinds of ways, and all sorts of problems can spring forth from the original one. Worry becomes anxiety. Uncertainty becomes fear.

Staying positive is damn hard work.

All of those wonderful self-care techniques are soul-nurturing for sure. I advocate all healthy wellness practices. Their benefits are undeniable. The catch is, they don't address the underlying and precipitating problems that are the cause of the stress. It's like chopping a weed with a lawn mower and leaving the root in the ground. The improvement is short-lived. The problem remains under the surface and before you know it, the problem and the stress are back, rearing their ugly heads. Then there's the chance that they will spread and before you know it, they've taken over the wonderfulness of you.

You want the problem to go away.

You need the stress to stop.

Where do you begin when the end isn't in sight?

You need a roadmap. You're looking for a starting place. A workable blueprint to build a solution. You need that blueprint to be a bespoke plan of action particular to who you are and one that checks all the boxes for your definition of happiness, fulfillment, and contentment. Not someone else's. You need that solution to support and elevate your life to the place you choose as success.

Where you are right now is a place on a dark road you don't know, and there are no directional signs. You want someone to tell you what to do next because you're too confused, or feel too lost, or are too exhausted to figure it out alone.

I want to be that someone. It's the reason I'm sharing the strategies that are the foundation of Coping Smart.

Why me? Because I developed these strategies out of a need in my personal life early on and continued to use them successfully in my professional approach. I've pursued my passion for understanding human behavior for decades. My educational path included an undergraduate degree in psychology and a Master of Counseling Psychology. I worked with individuals in a practice for a while before a move to another state for my husband's work. That relocation to a new community and the ages of my children prompted me to use my knowledge in a volunteer capacity to help others with what I knew. I founded and facilitated a grief support group in my church with a congregation of 10,000 members.

I discovered helping hurting people was my calling. That led me to question why some people are more resilient than others and if and how that resilience can be built.

Working with individuals on any problem has taught me that each person has a set of core values. You view those values through an individual and personal set of lenses that are determined by a unique set of factors. Everyone's formative experiences, family legacies, personalities, temperament, beliefs, and desires differ. Age and phase of life are factors in problem solving. That's why everyone deals with problems differently. No one theory or modality or motivational trend works for everyone. From my experience, I know that strategies that emphasize self-awareness and insight lay a foundation for success. I also realize how vital it is to acknowledge all those personal differences as well as the autonomy for people to choose for themselves what they define as workable. Like the differences in how people handle problems and stress, their ideas of happiness vary.

Happiness has become a commodity and an industry. There are hundreds of self-help books and podcasts that aim to tell you what you think and how you feel. Then they tell you what you *should* be feeling. I'm not one of those people and this isn't one of those books. I aim to help you discover true happiness for yourself, but I realize that the question of what makes you happy is secondary in a moment of difficulty. First, you've got to stop the fallout. The fog of confusion settles in as the problems and complications from a difficult situation occur. You can't see a way out. Often, you can't even see the road you're standing on. Clarity is at a premium. Isn't that what you're really looking for in this book? I know it's what I sought desperately when I was in distress. I needed honesty and specifics. I needed guidance and workable strategies to cope through the stress and get me to the other side of the problem where it would be behind me and the path forward would be clear. Once I discovered those successful strategies, I knew I had to share them with others.

I developed these strategies out of necessity. My father became critically ill when I was quite young. His constant hospitalizations meant he and my mother were gone much of the time leaving me as caregiver to my younger sister. I quickly learned to begin to think like an adult. I honed my problem-solving skills as I learned to assess situations and rely on my own judgement to make decisions for both myself and my little sister.

My father's prolonged illness changed him and all of us in ways that still affect the dynamics of our family. His death altered the trajectory of my life forever.

My mother felt her best option was to move back to her small hometown to raise my little sister who was still in grade school. She gave me the option to go with them or find an alternative. It was another adult decision I was asked to make. They moved to their new home and I left mine.

I became unofficially emancipated and with enough credits and the grades to gain early admission to college without graduating high school, my new life started. I was sixteen.

On my own, I continued to use my problem-solving and coping skills. I discovered my innate intuition and learned to trust it and to think critically. Becoming an adult seemed a natural part of the progression because I had been expected to be responsible for so long. It meant continuing to deal with all the coming-of-age issues without a guide or a safety net. Though it was an abbreviated adolescence and difficult, I think of this now as a gift of sorts. Navigating emotional issues and becoming self-reliant sparked my love of psychology. My self-taught strategies became the foundation of my life purpose and led me to write this book all these years later.

Learning to be resourceful became the cornerstone that supported me. I don't know how to not problem-solve. I can't imagine not sharing what I know works with others. In the tough times of my life, it has been the impetus for getting up off the floor and moving toward better.

I promised I would use what I had learned in service to others.

I promised to be the one who helps you discover the power you hold to overcome whatever problem presents in your life.

The one you point to and say, *she did it so can I.*

I tell you this not only as part of my story so you will know that I understand how life can be upended by difficulty, but as an example of what I came to know. But like anyone else, the unexpected turns in my life have been unpredictable and challenging again and again. I have since crashed on my life road twice in ways that could have defeated me. Because of the confidence my past successes at surviving and thriving had given me, devastation was not an option. I called on these successful strategies each time to be my headlights in the fog of confusion and heartache. That memory muscle of resilience was the direct result of Coping Smart.

I want to impart what I've learned from my experiences and my work with others. The basic principle is clear: When given the option to sink or swim, the only viable one for any hope of happiness is to swim. And that's only the beginning of the possibilities. The lane you pick and the stroke you choose is your decision as well. There is always at least one choice available to you. Then that choice leads to another and another and another. If you don't realize it yet, my hope is that you'll discover those choices are available to you in this moment and every moment a problem challenges your spirit. There are ways to cope through the stress. I know the peace that freedom from stress brings. That's what I want for you.

There *is* someone who understands. Let's talk about this problem you are facing, identify the source and the severity of the impact, clarify your options, and find ways to manage your emotions and stress. I'll use some ways for you to name what you're feeling and give it a shape. That's a coping strategy to give you some distance from emotions so you can get a handle on them. Metaphors are mighty when you're searching for meaning. I'll suggest making mental pictures of what a feeling would look like or a scenario that gives a visual for the situation to capture it in a way you can relate to it differently. These discoveries will give you a sense of success even before you find your workable solution. I'll acknowledge those successes along with you, not as generic affirmations, but as the sincerest validation I can offer for the efforts you'll be making and the progress and peace you'll achieve.

I'll ask you questions that will serve as road signs to show you where you've been and help you decide where you want to go next. I'll help you develop a blueprint to build a stronger you. I'll share some stories about a few of the folks I've helped cope through a problem in a way that illustrates a concept to you while it honors them and maintains confidentiality.

Cited studies, charts and graphs are great academic references, but when you're in the middle of struggling with a difficulty you want uncomplicated strategies for relief, not statistics. I'll avoid clichés and only use quotes that will give you clarity, not vague positivity. You need and deserve more.

I've written this book as if we are sitting together somewhere, just the two of us talking about you and what you're going through in this moment. You have my full attention. I know your family may be the last place you'd go for this particular problem. They wouldn't fully understand, or they'd never let you live it down, or they would become angry at anyone who caused you pain and never forgive them even if you did. You might be too embarrassed or ashamed to let them know what you're going through. You can't talk to your partner if they're part of the problem. Your friends love you, but they're weary from hearing about it over and over. They all want you to be okay. They mean well, but they need you to be happy and move on, so they can feel better. That has probably left you feeling even more alone.

I've been in a place where it was so dark, and I was so scared, I couldn't say it out loud, because it would pull everyone else in my life who depended on me into the black hole with me. I couldn't risk that.

I had to go it alone.

I don't want that for you.

That's why I offer my counsel. That's why I wrote this book.

Let's get you back in control, stronger and equipped to overcome the problem, moving forward out from under the stress and toward your workable solution. Think about the word *work* in a new way. I won't ask you to "do the work" like many experts and therapists require. Instead I'll ask you to take action toward change that will bring about the relief you are looking for. This will help you feel less burdened and more in charge. That's what this book is all about. I want to guide you to discover all that you have within you.

It's time to start Coping Smart.

TELL ME ABOUT YOU

Instructions for living a life: / Pay attention. / Be astonished. / Tell about it.

—Mary Oliver

CHAPTER ONE:

YOUR LEGACY

Something happened. It changed things. It changed everything. Maybe you want to change the situation. You keep asking yourself how this happened.

You don't understand. You want to understand. You *need* to understand.

You don't know where to begin.

Here's what I know. Understanding leads to clarity. Clarity leads to insight. Insight leads to knowledge. Knowledge leads to power. Power leads to freedom. The cumulative dividend of that chain reaction is the place of peace you're seeking.

I know right now that sounds like oversimplification of what's troubling you. It also looks like a lot of steps to feel better. You need immediate relief from the stress that's sitting on your chest right now. Look again at the straightforward line these concepts make on the page. It can be that way in your application of the strategies in this book. You're overwhelmed with a problem and the stress has you in an uncomfortable place. The stress is messing with your mind and has you in a state of confusion. You need to break it down in a way that makes all the parts make sense.

When you want wisdom and insight as badly as you want
to breathe, it is then you shall have it.

—Socrates

Wow. Right? Wisdom is a lofty term for successful problem solving. Isn't that what you are really looking for? You've got a problem in your life that's threatening your happiness and challenging your ability to cope. The stress is killing you.

Why this?

Why you?

To truly be *wise* so that you aren't bruised by the hard knocks of life, you must begin with the *"whys"* of you. Why do you feel this sadness? Why are you unhappy? Why are certain things pushbuttons for your anger or resentment? Why is this stuff always happening to you? Why are you the one who ended up hurt?

If the first quote doesn't feel relevant to you, try this one.

Many of the truths we cling to depend greatly on our own point of view.

—Obi-Wan Kenobi

Not everyone thinks the same. I know that's hard to accept. You operate from your own logic and often assume everyone else believes, or at least should believe, the same. It's the reason why when someone does something you think is foolish or ill-advised, you ask the proverbial question. *What were they thinking?* You can't understand why they did what they did. You wouldn't have handled it that way.

Each person has opinions and varying degrees of knowledge about life based on their experiences. Everyone's experiences differ, sometimes widely. That's why you're often disappointed by the people in your life. They don't think in the same way and therefore don't act and react the same way you do. It's hard for you to get into their mindset if you have no similar reference in your own life. You can't find harmony when the singers aren't in tune. You might not know their song at all.

When a problem presents, a solution is needed.

You're looking for a solution right now.

The process of Coping Smart begins with the first moment you decide to take a look at where you began to be you. You might be saying, Becki, I don't want to talk about my feelings about my domineering mother, how I never got my father's approval, or that my sister was the favorite. It's too painful to think about how the drama of divorce, or the fallout of addiction, or the tragic death of a parent or a sibling wrecked my childhood. What does that have to do with the problem I'm facing now?

This moment of reflection won't be as unnecessary as you might think in your hurry to stop hurting.

It won't take long.

It doesn't have to be as uncomfortable as you may anticipate.

It matters. You may even get some real relief from the hold your past may have on you by stepping back and seeing where the emotions have taken root. With some effort you can weed that garden for good.

I'm the last person to ask you to dwell in the past. That's a place of much danger. It can be a siren call to despair if you revisit it too often or too long. Worse yet, if you decide to stay. But it's a fabulous place to start on a journey of understanding. Think of it as your post position in the starting gate in The Kentucky Derby, the green flag at The Indy 500, the starting block in the Olympic events, or even the *Start Here* square on a board game. You're using it as a marker of where to begin to understand that you're in this situation because of where you've been. It's the road that led to here. It will determine the path to where you want to go from here. You can only know where you're going if you acknowledge where you started and how far you have to go. Your starting line might be further back than others, but the road is open.

So, take one of those deep breaths everyone has been telling you to do, and for a few moments, let's talk about where you began.

Home, the first place you lived and the people who were around you, is the soil of every human's beginning. It is where the seed of you was planted. The level of care you received determined how well you grew. Not only physically, but also emotionally.

Who cared for you and about you, how they demonstrated love or hate, how they fought and made or didn't make amends, lied or told the truth, showed honor or disrespect, gave affection or withheld it, did harm or good, lived connected or disengaged, coped or crumbled, and all their other behaviors and values or lack of shaped the foundation of what you believed about how the world works and how everyone in it lives. It may be what you still believe.

It's the foundation of your belief system until and unless you change it.

> *All you know is what you know.*
> —Richard R. Pickett

That's a quote, not from my academic studies, but from my husband who is the source of much elegant simple wisdom. Let me take a moment to note a good life lesson here. Worthy messages are all around you if you listen. Never underestimate their value or dismiss the source.

I couldn't agree with Richard more. Your understanding is limited by your knowledge.

It's the perfect explanation for the huge spectrum of human behavior. Some of us get better instruction and direction early on, and some don't. It's like the quality of any form of education.

You know what you've been taught.

Children mimic and mirror what they see as a method of learning. When a parent is teaching and encouraging a child to speak, the parent holds up an object and repeats the corresponding word until the child echoes it back. When parents want a baby to learn how to wave good-bye, they gesture as they demonstrate as if to say, *Do as I do.* When urging a toddler to walk the parent first shows the child how to take steps offering cues to say *This is the way it's done. I am showing you how. I know what I'm doing.*

Trust me, they say with non-verbal commands.

You did.

You were watching, you followed their example, and you trusted them to always have your best interests at heart. If you were fortunate to have savvy parents, you received great instruction. If not, you may find yourself lacking the coping skills you need. You may have also assumed a worldview that is counterproductive for true emotional equilibrium. To some people the world is a cruel, hard place to be suffered. To others it's a place where they feel entitled to all good fortune. Fearfulness, pessimism, and chronic disappointment are mindsets to some as boldness, optimism, and hopefulness are to others. The emotional climate in your early home determined an automatic setting on your emotional thermostat.

Because you're searching for ways to cope with the situation you are facing in your life right now, take a moment to remember how your parents or caretakers in your early life reacted to problems. From simple frustrations to tragedies, how well did they cope? How did they fail to cope effectively?

Juliet was a woman I worked with on discovering how her legacy had shaped her coping style. Her father was a dynamic high-achiever who worked in sales. His powers of persuasion were the key to his success. They were also pervasive in the way he dealt with his family. He thrived on being the center of attention and captivating everyone's cooperation. He did not tolerate resistance well, especially at home.

Juliet's mom was very talented in her own right but put her career aspirations on hold when Juliet and her siblings were born. She was a devoted wife who believed the best way to have harmony was to take the path of least resistance. Her coping skills consisted of compliance and avoidance. Later in life those morphed into rewriting history to fit her story of what she wanted to believe and what she wanted others to believe her husband and family were.

Juliet's parents had a dynamic where her father was the one always in control and her mother deferred to him. She insisted the children do the same without question.

The control I'm talking about here was not abusive in any way but it was influential in forming Juliet's view of how relationships work. She was taught by example to suppress her own ideas and to follow a lead. Her mother's coping choice was always to allow her husband to shine even if it meant dimming her own light.

In Juliet's marriage the same dynamic was in place. She avoided conflict with her husband and her children at all costs. She denied herself permission to say no to anyone. Her goal became to serve as the peacemaker and compliance ambassador for everyone else's happiness. She mirrored her mother's relationship style without realizing it. She had become very dissatisfied in her life and had begun to suffer symptoms of anxiety and depression.

The problem was she couldn't name it. She knew she was unhappy and had lost much of her enthusiasm and joy but was unaware of the root cause. When Juliet began to question her legacy, she asked her mother to explain her reasons for the ways she chose to cope. Her mother refused to acknowledge the reality of her behavior and that of Juliet's father. At that point denial had become Juliet's mom's coping mechanism. It was a legacy of dysfunction.

All of this became a template for Juliet. Only through examining her legacy as the source of the pattern of her choices, she came to accept that she was making herself sick trying to insure everyone's happiness. Change was then possible.

Another client Bryan had a problem with being the one who was controlling. He grew up in a single parent home where his mother dictated his every move. She told him how to do everything. She was constantly telling him who his friends should be and how he should feel and behave. Bryan adored her but he began to push back with his own desire to be in control. It led to a major rift in their relationship.

Later on, his need to be in charge and unwillingness to compromise affected Bryan's ability to maintain a happy relationship. When he looked at his legacy in our sessions, he revealed that when he was six-years old his younger brother had drowned at the age of three. His mother had never healed from that tragedy. Her guilt at not preventing her child's death though not founded in reality was her perception. She channeled that grief and guilt into a need to control her remaining child's life. She equated control with protection.

It became clear to Bryan he was carrying on that legacy. He was trying to keep bad things from happening. He was attempting to avoid having his life altered again by an accident. He was able to shift his attention from fear and control to trusting the possibility of joyful surprises in life. Then he could believe that sharing it with someone equally was an asset not a liability.

I believe resentment and the miseries of family dysfunction pool and stagnate into black waters. Those murky depths threaten family harmony. Any time two or more members interact in a dysfunctional family, they stir up the unresolved muck and create a whirlpool of negativity that pulls everyone involved down. You spend time together trying to keep your head above the water. You get exhausted from treading. The raw memories of the deficits loom way larger than any sized happiness remembered. This accounts for miserable holidays and other family gatherings so many people endure.

Jokes about family dysfunction are the backbone of comedy. If you're fortunate, your family may have a few quirks in the way they relate, and you can appreciate the humor. If not, there may be a serious and destructive pathology that can cripple your ability to enjoy your family to the fullest. The worse scenario is it may prevent you from doing the same with your children unless you actively resist. History repeats itself without focused intent to do otherwise. It's all relative with relatives.

Some people can distinguish and even complain about it, but many don't even realize they have adopted their family dysfunction as their norm. That's the pervasive side effect of the "all you know is what you know" theory we talked about.

I worked with a client, Brooke, who grew up in a family that dealt with any and all confrontation large or small by shouting at each other. Screaming was an accepted form of communication in the rules of engagement for conflict in their home. They had an unspoken agreement by the environment set by their parents' example where they said what they wanted to say, and no hard feelings remained. When the fight was over it was truly over. It made for a very loud home, but it worked for them.

When Brooke brought her fiancé Jake home from college to meet her family, he was stunned at the level of what he perceived as hostility. He couldn't believe how they yelled at each other and the unkind things they said. He knew from their experiences as a couple that Brooke could get loud at times when they fought, but he had a tendency to shut down and become quiet, so it had never escalated to another level. He dismissed it in his mind as something that only happened in that house when Brooke's family was together.

Once they were married and the normal disagreements of cohabitation arose and conflict was more prominent, the couple found their modes of fighting were incompatible. Brooke screamed her emotions. Jake felt wounded by her words. He felt she was callous. She couldn't understand why he was so sensitive. You can imagine the turmoil it created when they had children. In an otherwise workable marriage, this couple had reached a place of incompatibility that threatened their family.

They could have let the conflict infect their home and their opposing styles could have become irreconcilable. I challenged them to take a step back to locate the origin of the discord between them. Once they had insight into their differences and realized they were stylistic rather than philosophical, it gave them a roadmap to getting back on track with specific intentional changes and compromise. They simply had learned contrasting emotional styles. They decided to make a new legacy for themselves and their children.

Then there are the families who carelessly inflict pain without regard to impact. Unchecked words are weapons. Hurting each other is an acceptable behavior to them. This is often also the breeding ground of labels. A parent calls you lazy or stupid. You're less than in one way or another. One child is the smart one. One is the pretty one. One child is the popular one. One is the geek. One child is the dream kid. One is the troublemaker. You believe what you're told by the most important people in your life whose authority you trust without question. This labeling also sets up resentment and jealousy among children in the home. But worse, low self-esteem often originates with early association with home environment. As your view of the world is shaped by your early experiences, your self-view is molded in the same way. Validation is crucial, and the lack of it is devastating. You trust that what your parents say is true. When you don't hear affirmations you hear volumes in that silence and believe you aren't worthy. They are the only experts you know as a child.

You've probably heard of a theory of psychology that references self-fulfilling prophecy. Basically, you become what you say you are. My addendum to that would be, unless you work at it, you become what you hear others say you are. All you know is what you know in the beginning, but at any moment in your life you have the opportunity to choose differently. It's never too late to declare who you are and to stake your claim on the life you want. Never.

A perfect example of this was a young man I helped once who struggled with extreme jealousy within his family. Collin was attractive, articulate, and clever enough with a quip to have been in stand-up comedy. He was also quite a talented artist, though it was his older brother who was the designated artistic one by their parents. They made sacrifices to send his brother to an expensive art institute while this young man was always in trouble at school and dropped out of college. When I met Collin, he was married with two very small children. The problem was his temper. He was oppositional to the point of being belligerent where his parents and especially his brother were concerned. Whenever they were in the same room, Collin's anger erupted. His wife had lived through several years of miserable family meals at her in-laws and disrupted holidays. Once they started having children of their own, she decided she wanted them to visit their grandparents' home without the emotional toll.

Collin acknowledged that his children deserved that. He realized how detrimental his behavior was to them. After going over his family dynamics and identifying the nature of the problem as his resentment of not being recognized for his value, I asked him to describe what would happen if he made the necessary emotional changes to shift that dynamic. His answer was quick and clear. Without hesitation, he answered my question with a question. If he was no longer the black sheep of the family who would he be? He couldn't conceptualize how to be anyone other than the person his family said he was, and he had accepted and adopted it as his identity. It was truly the way he felt. It made my heart hurt for him. His potential had been stifled and his life derailed unnecessarily. Words were the only things that stood in his way. He had accepted them as a declaration of his destiny.

Parents or guardians create your first environment and set your perception about life. If they call each other or the others in your home disrespectful names, or inflict emotional hurt without remorse, or disregard others, the effect is imprinted on you. Conversely, what they don't say when you need to hear it can be just as damaging. Confidence is strongest when it is instilled early. Words form powerful forces.

Much unhappiness has come from things left unsaid.
—Leo Tolstoy

Let's talk about your early family. I believe that, for gaining clarity, asking the right question is often many times more important than giving the right answers. It's like playing *Jeopardy*. You don't score until you ask the correct question.

- What roles did gender play? The example you grew up with about how men are expected to act or what a woman's place is in the family hierarchy are pervasive influences on every aspect of your worldview. It forms what you perceive as acceptable and desirable for your place in your life. Even roles that benefit one partner but slight the other can be harmful examples. If one hides their light so another one shines, or one gives without reciprocation, the precedent may continue.

- Have you repeated unhealthy relationship roles later in your life? This comes to the choice part of learning from your early family experience. This is where disappointment can begin to erode relationships, children's self-esteem is diminished, the chain of domestic violence begins, emotional abuse takes hold, infidelity cancels trust, and where much familial misery continues to infect and diminish families generationally and hinder their potential for harmony and shared happiness.

- Have you used your family legacy as a template by replicating the favorable things or by avoiding repetition of the unfavorable aspects?

- What values were present in your upbringing? This is where the validation for the virtues of honesty, respect, empathy, compassion, and service come into existence in your personal development. This is where resourcefulness, ambition, integrity, responsibility, and honor become—or fail to become—permanent fixtures on your personal landscape. Like any measurement of effort, the potential outcome is directly dependent on the quality of the source. The output is proportional to the input.

- What values from your early development do you still honor and protect?

- What values were missing?

- How are you making up for that deficit now?

- Identify the problems that were in your early life.

- How did your parents or guardians receive or reject your early attempts to problem-solve?

- Did they praise you for your strategies or did they admonish your ways to problem solve?

- Did they draw a distinct line between constructive criticism and shame?

- How did that constructive criticism help you?

- If you were given shame, how did it affect you?

- Is that shame an influence in your life still?

- Did they allow you to handle problems yourself or did they intercept or intervene?

- How did that effect you at the time?

- How is it still effecting you?

- If it was a factor, how do you believe your parents' overprotection was meant to spare you the pain of embarrassment or failure?

- Was it more self-serving and meant to spare them embarrassment?

- If they didn't try to help, was their lack of involvement when you encountered problems negligent?

- Did they fail to help you when you needed them most?

- Will you consider your legacy in these ways to help guide you in your own parenting experience and create a new legacy for your children?

This is where you learned not only by example, but by an emotional osmosis of sorts. The association of good or bad responses to stress and favorable or unfavorable ways to deal with problem situations seeps into your core and remains unless you decide to change it.

All these components of your family legacy are integral to your coping skill level and problem-solving success. They matter. They hold much in the way of insight once you identify them. Acknowledging them can boost your confidence in your ability to cope through a problem. Conversely, recognizing the deficits supplies information so you can focus on acquiring the skills you need.

Discovering these influences offers an additional bonus.

Insight is the recognition that activates motivation.

What moves you?

Why you do what you do, think what you think, and feel what you feel is the substance of motivation.

True wisdom is using that insight to understand why you behave in certain ways. As importantly, true wisdom that comes with insight of your behavior provides an understanding of the motivations of others. What moves them to do what they do? Will you make the effort to see what experiences shaped them and where they are coming from emotionally?

Maybe your constant nudging reminders to your husband feel like his mother's reprimands. What if your wife's insistence that you're romantically attracted to your co-worker is based on her father's abandonment of her and her mother when she was young? Maybe your insecurity in a social setting is due to your mother's criticism when you were a teen.

Consider how your perception of intent is colored by your experiences.

Once you stop to examine your emotional legacy, you will see the effect. Then you can rectify it. Once you forgive the deficit, you might be able to extend that understanding to the people in your life who may have screwed up. Even if they can't see it or they never change, you will free yourself by recognizing it has little or nothing to do with you or what you did. It's not about you. Don't own it.

So why does all of this matter? Before you can ask anyone else in your life to understand who you are, where you are coming from emotionally, and what you expect and want to happen, you must know the answers to those questions yourself. You can't expect someone else to know something about you that you don't know yourself.

The past matters only as a cornerstone anchor of the foundation of your life. You get to choose what kind of life, what that life will look like, how strong it is against the storms.

Lay that stone in place and lay it to rest.

You can build on it and continue with like stones or choose new ones to change the pattern to a more desirable one. It's your choice.

I caution you to also consider that this understanding what shapes and motivates any behavior isn't always about why. Why is a magical answer we often seek but sometimes never find. When available, it can provide a sense of satisfaction that there's a logical and discoverable reason. That's wonderful when it happens. Unfortunately, why isn't a given. The quest for it can distract and disappoint you. I urge you not to spend too much time being taken down by the undertow of asking an unanswerable question. A clear reason why can contribute to your insight, but despite its allure to assuage natural human curiosity, it isn't necessary for your healing unless you set that standard.

Often you must release the need for why and let the next step be *what*.

So, I encourage you to see your early life through your older and wiser eyes now. Step back, and mentally observe what went on there. Distance from it with an exercise I use. Think of it as a reality show starring someone else that you're telling a friend about.

Here are some things to ask yourself so that the storyline is clear:

How would you describe the characters? In casting your show, think about who would play the parts of the members of your family. Describe the actor playing you.

- How do the players effectively or ineffectively interact? This is where your perception comes in. How you use your memories to design the scenes on your storyboard will determine the characters' actions. Motivation is a great revealer of perception.

- What motivates the characters? This is where you show the dynamics of how they feel about each other. It's also where you identify how you see yourself and your relationships.

- What's the emotional climate? Here's where the drama kicks up. This is the part about who did what that made whomever feel the way they felt and choose how they reacted. Here's where you get to show how you felt about living in that environment.

- What's predictable in the action? Can the viewers see what's coming next episode to episode by the characters' past behavior? Does that help you see the patterns of your life?

- What patterns of behavior keep showing up? Can each member of the cast be described by what they do over and over again? Can you see your own repeated behaviors?

- What situations are the most compelling? Here's another place you get out those memories that are the most vivid and impactful to you.

- What are the possible scenarios if the characters changed their behavior? This is dream world time where you get to consider the ways things might have been different. Then you can see how legacy can be changed. You have the power to change it going forward.

- What would you change about any one character? How could you facilitate and impact that change for them? Wishful thinking can be converted to a worthy goal and often be a path to insight.

- What would you change about the character that is you? This is where you examine the power you have to initiate change by starting with the only thing you can control. You.

- If you posted a review online about this show and its characters, what would your critique of their story be? This is the reality check. Look at your legacy not in judgment but with compassion for all the players—including yourself.

Did it help to think of your early life that way? Sometimes distance from the emotion can actually bring it more into focus. This is a great coping skill.

Ok, you've examined the things in your early life that shaped you and may still be influencing your behavior. That's all about the other people in your beginning. Now let's talk about you.

CHAPTER TWO:

YOUR WIRING

Today you are you, that is truer than true. There is no one alive who is youer than you.

—Dr. Seuss

Imagine you're filling out an online personal profile. You're asked to describe your personality. What would you write? If it helps, think for a moment about being around the corner in a place where you can overhear a conversation between two people you know well. They're talking about you. What adjectives do you hear when they describe your temperament?

You are who you are, but why?

The debates about nature versus nurture have been ongoing since ancient times. I won't go into the history and the countless studies and the shifting of prevailing trends toward each school of thought. Are you the way you are because you're genetically coded to be a Pollyanna who sees rainbows and unicorns or a Chicken Little who only sees the sky as falling? Is that temper that erupts from you in a moment's notice exactly like it does in your mother due to DNA, or because she was the first role model in your life, and you mirror her behavior? You may have the same quirky sense of humor as your grandfather, or get your feelings hurt easily like your cousin, or procrastinate like your aunt, or shut down when frustrated like your dad, or be passive-aggressive like your sister.

Working with individuals on problem solving, being a partner in a marriage for decades, raising two children into adulthood, being a grandmother to two teens plus a grade-schooler, and leading as a boss to a range of ages, I have come to understand that people have internal wiring that is their default setting for personality and temperament. Whether the origin of that preset was genetically placed or influenced by environment, for the purpose of examining coping skills and problem solving, *why* isn't as important as *what*.

You possess traits that are as identifiably you as your eye color or height. Those are the tools, the ingredients, the materials, the components, the specifics you've been given to work with. You decide what to do with them where your behavior and attitude are concerned.

Personality is usually described as the "what "and "why" of what you do, whereas temperament is described as the "how" or "way" you do something. The term personality is used to describe a behavior type and temperament. It's your style of behaving.

The important thing now is to think about what makes you who you are. Aspects like being introverted or extroverted, impulsive or cautious, optimistic or pessimistic, suspicious or trusting, practical or spontaneous are descriptors of distinct personality types. In terms of the way you are "wired", are you quick to anger or a slow burn, a morning person or night owl, a leader or follower, an instigator or peacemaker, easy-going or moody? All of those factors play a part in how you approach problems.

I have no intention of telling you which of these is more desirable. You already know this for yourself. It depends on you and what you want your life, your career, and your relationships to look like. Oftentimes it's finding the place where your personality fits or the person who is compatible. If a personality trait continually gets in your way of achieving your personal goals, you may have to consider an adjustment. Sometimes it requires a totally new way of thinking to bring about a complete change in behavior. Others need only a small shift in thought to achieve the tweak you need.

It's always possible. Human behavior is malleable. Change is a constant variable. That's the foundation of behavior modification therapies to lose weight, stop smoking, conquer phobias, manage anger, or break any pattern you consider a bad habit or undesirable trait. Note that word *modification*. That can mean a change due to stopping the behavior altogether or change through adapting, adjusting, or altering. It doesn't always require an all or nothing response. This can take away the pressure to define success as total change and failure as anything else. Recognizing a need to make a change is the first big step. Any movement toward the desired change is worthy of your recognition of it as an accomplishment.

Honor yourself for it.

The decision to make a change in your behavior is an ever-open opportunity. There's no expiration date or statute of limitations. The strategies for changing your behavior are cognitive.

That simply means what you think about you bring about.

Before you shut down here, I know that sounds like I'm saying that what's happening is your fault. I'm not at all. This isn't about blame. It's about empowerment. You're always thinking. That never stops. You have thousands of thoughts every day. Thousands. That's a lot of work on top of all the other systems operations you don't have to worry about because your marvelous brain does it for you. Your mind is always thinking about something. That being true, then doesn't it make the most sense to have those thoughts be pleasant or productive? Better still, wouldn't it be beneficial to give your brain both of those instead of worry, anxiety, fear, and doubt?

You know you can interrupt a thought if you want. You can even make it go away. You've done it before. You're going along doing something and an unpleasant thought comes into your head. You replace it and think of something else. Haven't you been in the middle of doing something when someone asks you a question that you don't have the time or inclination to answer? Didn't you answer by saying you can't think about that right now? You can compartmentalize your thoughts. You can prioritize them. You can recall or create thoughts on command. Sounds like a lot of control is available where your thoughts are concerned. That's what behavior modification is all about. You're more in charge than you might feel right now.

Action begins with a thought. You get to choose the action, your behavior. That means you are in control of your ability to change. Think about an undesirable behavior. You can form educated thoughts based on facts separate from your feelings and make a deliberate decision to act in a certain way in a certain situation.

First you think.

Then you do.

Sounds simple. The hard part is continuing the change long enough and consistently enough to bring about and sustain the desired result for the long term. That's a fancy way of saying you've got to keep it up to make change last.

Let's go over that again. These questions and suggestions will give you some perspective on behavior modification.

- Identify what behavior you want to change.

- What can you do differently that will bring about the change and the result that you want?

- What facts support your theory for change?

- Are you willing to make the decision to change your behavior?

- Are you certain that the desire to change is yours and not the result of trying to please someone else or fit their mold?

- Will you commit to the action necessary to change?

- If you're going to do something, why not do something that will bring a good result?

- Will you commit to being consistent with the new behavior?

- Refrain from blame when you backslide. Setbacks are inevitable. They're more easily overcome if you expect them. You don't have to start completely over every time you slip back into the old behavior. That's a defeatist attitude that will leave you feeling as if you've failed. Instead, start again where you left off. Measure success by effort, not only by end results.

- Replace blame with rewarding yourself every time you're successful.

- Resist old patterns by sustaining a new perspective. New behavior requires new thoughts.

- Instead of feeling overwhelmed, will you choose to think of it as a step forward toward feeling better? You're going to feel something. Wouldn't it be great for those emotions to be good ones?

You behave yourself into situations every day and with everything you do. If what you're doing isn't getting the results you want, then choose different behavior.

You can do it.

What you can't change is someone else's behavior.

Let me repeat that.

You can't change someone else's behavior.

You've heard it over and over, but still somewhere deep inside you believe if you do enough you can get them to change. You believe with all your heart that if you do everything right or if you can get them to love you enough then you can get them to act or think differently.

Listen to me. You can beg, threaten, pray, cajole, shame, coax, bribe, humiliate, rage, inspire, suggest, or encourage, but you can't change someone else's behavior. It is their choice. It is only their choice. Notice the word *choice*. Don't believe it if someone tells you they can't help how they behave. Just like you, they're capable of change if they really desire it. They have to want to change. You wanting it isn't enough. It's their decision alone.

Here's some really important good news. The other people in your life are not in control of *your* choices concerning them. You decide your threshold of acceptance and your deal-breakers where their behavior is concerned.

The same is true of what you accept from yourself. Like breaking any pattern, it's hard, but worth it. It's also an ongoing, long-term commitment. You're willing to make those kinds of promises to someone else. Do it for yourself. A lot of modern advice talks about the need for you to practice self-love.

Think of establishing your deal-breakers as the truest form of self-love.

Note it as a worthy goal. Make it your motto.

I am the master of my fate: I am the captain of my soul.
—William Ernest Henley

Wow. Sounds bold, doesn't it? There's nothing wishful about those words. They aren't abstract positivity affirmations. They're definitive statements. In the same way you can think yourself into behaving, you can think yourself into believing. Isn't that what a belief is? It's a thought or an idea that you hold dear. You're convinced.

Imagine yourself as a sculptor, author, architect or maestro—you are in control of you. Tell yourself you're in charge. Tell yourself again and again. Tell yourself until you believe it. Make it a conviction.

So, that's the reality of behavior. It isn't some involuntary response or random act. It's a choice. Yours alone. It's also a step forward out of this uncomfortable place of stress. In the same way your thoughts are ongoing, your movement through your life is constant. Do you want to step back, putting you further from your idea of happiness? Do you want to march in place surrounded by stress, getting nowhere? Or do you want to go forward? You're in charge. You pick.

Now, let's talk about your emotions. Those feelings that we allow to govern our behavior can be powerful. Do they come over you or are you in control where they're concerned?

Emotions are the catalysts that start the chain reaction of how we act.

How many times have you said that you can't help the way you feel?

You meant it.

A co-worker disagreed with you and you felt invalidated. Your partner chose a night with friends instead of date night with you, and you felt rejected. Your child was defiant, and you felt resentful. Your parent was critical of you, and you felt dejected. Being ignored by others made you feel invisible and unworthy.

Emotions come in all sizes. Some simply color your view and some rock your world. They come upon you in what seems to be another involuntary reaction when they register in your brain. Your emotions are part of your wiring. But they are subject to examination and change.

I could go into all sorts of explanation of the neurobiology and neuroscience of emotions and the brain and the limbic system, but my experience with people who are looking for coping skills in the middle of a difficulty has been that such scientific information isn't what they were looking for. It's probably not what you're looking for in this moment. You know that your emotions can be marvelous and welcomed. They can also be counterproductive and undesirable.

You may believe you are wired to be emotional or unemotional because your relatives are one or the other. That propensity may certainly be real, but you can decide whether to be a part of that pattern or take deliberate steps to change it. Think of an old house. The wiring is no longer adequate for what you want. You're adding an addition onto the house and adjustments have to be made for it to fulfill your current and future needs.

Maybe it's time to consider an upgrade to your connection to the power source of you. If there are things about yourself that you want to change, you can. If there are things you do that are interfering with the quality of your relationships, then you can stop doing them or find a more productive behavior. Maybe what once worked for you no longer does now that the situation has changed. Consider these questions to find out:

What personality traits of yours do value in yourself? No humility here or self-deprecation. Brag. Find your swagger. Pat yourself on the back. Vote for yourself.

- Which ones do you wish were different? No self-incrimination or condemnation. Be merciful. Be constructive.

- What personality traits in you do other people consistently point out as favorable? Again, no humility here. Toot your own horn.

- What personality traits in you do other people consistently point out as undesirable? Be objective.

- Can you see merit in what they say? Take how you feel about them out of the picture and look at the facts like a student on a mission to learn.

- What results of your wiring do you believe play a part in your ability or inability to manage problems? Are you impatient by nature? Are you a drama queen?

- What effect do you believe your temperament has on the quality of your relationships?

- Do the people in your life act as though they benefit from interaction with you or is it a negative experience?

- Do you think an adjustment on your part would improve your relationships? Reality check here. Consider if a shift in you could enhance your life.

- What about your wiring is a positive influence on your life? Concentrate on your attributes. Honoring them will increase their scope.

- What about your personality do you think is an obstacle to achieving your goals? This is time to be real. Honesty is the start of self-improvement.

- Is finding constructive ways to re-wire your behavior necessary to finding a solution to this problem you are facing?

- What personality traits in others do you admire? This is what I call the Theory of Proven Success. You don't have to guess what works. Someone else has already done the work for you. Paint by numbers.

- Which of your personality traits do others admire? This takes the question about what personality traits others find favorable in you a step further. Aspire to *inspire*.

- Can you take a moment to focus on your positive traits and honor them as assets to lean on as you cope through difficulty?

Recognizing your core wiring is essential for understanding the difficulties in your life. It's the starting place for those why, how, and what questions you're asking. Acknowledging your default settings is the beginning of true self-awareness. It's where change begins, and you begin to change. Don't settle for *this is how it is* when there is a better *this is how it could be*. This is another opportunity to start getting your power back. You may feel helpless about a lot of things, but your behavior and your viewpoint are always at your command. This is where you can truly begin to feel getting stronger against the problem you're facing even if it looks bigger than you feel.

To get started changing and taking charge of your emotions, do this simple exercise. Instead of asking yourself *how does this situation make you feel* , ask *how do you feel about this situation?* See the difference? In the first question, you're giving the situation control over your emotion. In the second you're declaring your right to choose your reaction.

I know all this talk of change sounds like a lot to think about. I know you're tired and that may be more than you can require of yourself at the moment. But remember, at the very beginning of this book you said you wanted something to change. You agreed that you need things to change because you can't go on living with all this stress. I want that for you. That's why I'm telling you about the ways change is possible. I want you to see that despite how low you feel, you're still in charge. You still have control of you. Hang on to that. Even if you can't embrace the scope of your power to bring about the change you desire, take a tiny step toward believing it may be possible.

If you can't change it, change your attitude.
—Maya Angelou

CHAPTER THREE:

YOUR LOCATION

You're not sure where to go next or how to get there. Let's say you're using your GPS to get directions. You could envision a roadmap as well. The first piece of information needed to find out how to get somewhere you desire to go is your current location. You can't find a direction without it. The satellite needs your exact position to begin tracking the route.

This life road you're on is a continuum. A sequence of markers defines position on that continuity. Where you are in your life, your location, is a huge factor in coping with stress along the way. What I'm talking about here is not actually a physical location but a timeline location. Your age, your lifestyle, your career placement, your relationships, and your responsibilities are the input to consider. What has happened to you and the types of obstacles you have encountered so far make a huge difference in calculating the route to your desired destination. The scarcity of obstacles matters as well. Some people have what seems like more than their share of difficulty early on. Some are spared those experiences until later. Some situations come only when you reach a certain phase of life. Emotional maturity and experience that come with the phases of your life provide their own set of signposts for coping through difficulty. They are factors in the "fork in the road" choices. They will determine your direction.

The factors we've talked about so far, your legacy and your wiring, influence your experiences. Together they will determine which direction you take when those either-or choices appear on your road. It's like when the GPS gives you alternate routes to a destination. Some get you there the fastest, others more scenic, others avoid traffic or construction. All lead to where you want to go, but you choose the course. In that choice, you are in charge of your next experiences. See how you are in control even when you feel the opposite? I want you to get that feeling down inside your gut.

It may feel differently in the moment, but things don't simply happen to you randomly. Events and situations are set into motion by many factors.

Now let's talk about your location. I'll explain the different places you might be in at this moment. You might be tempted to skip parts that aren't applicable to you right now. I do encourage you to read about each of them, as it may help you understand where you were before that led you to where you are now, and give you clarity about something you might not have realized affected you then that continues to affect you.

Here's the most important reason to take a look at all of them. Even if I'm talking about a phase that doesn't describe your current location, it may help you understand the point of view of the other people in your life who are a part of your current experience.

No one exists and functions in this world totally alone. The problem you face involves someone else in some way. It may concern a child, teen, young adult, adult parent, peer, spouse, partner, or friend. They may be much like you, or they may be in a different phase of life and location than you. Either way, it's vital to identify and acknowledge that. If you read about the different locations as I discuss them, you'll be prompted to dig a little deeper than what you might see on the surface and begin to relate to them in a new way. This can be a great kick-starter for change and another opportunity for you to take charge in a stressful situation.

One of the most effective coping skills is empathy. We'll talk about empathy a lot as we go along. Grasping another person's point of view when they are part of the problem is crucial for stress management and problem solving. That insight is exactly what you need for a workable solution.

Childhood

From infancy, behavior affects results in getting basic human needs met. You cry and someone changes your diaper, feeds you, burps you, or covers your cold extremities. Simple cause and effect.

Learning the value of cooperation comes next as a means to having your needs and desires accommodated. You learn to repeat behavior that gets you what you want.

In healthy development, children learn to seek approval by merit. They behave in a way that elicits praise and reward. It's a classic win-win. Conversely, if they learn the only way to garner your attention is through inappropriate behavior then that will be reinforced. You set up which behavior the child chooses. Your response is a child's only cue. Children want to be praised. They crave it. They also want to be noticed and validated. When they can't get a parent's attention with acceptable behavior, kids quickly learn that acting out gets it almost every time. Any reaction, even if it's punishment, becomes their goal. Why would they want to get into trouble? It seems illogical, but when you consider that any type and amount of attention that they get from you is paramount to their self-esteem, then it's easier to understand their motivation.

One of life's earliest emotional milestones is learning to get along with others. Conflict resolution is one of the first interpersonal skills required of everyone. How conflict is managed in the home is a child's only example. Parents' reactions to each other when they disagree and their anger management style with a child is crucial to their development. Even if they are very young, remember that they're watching your every move. You may think they are too little to understand, but they hear everything. Although they may not comprehend the words, they're hyper-sensitive to your tone and demeanor. Every child is born with a built-in emotional barometer. They possess a sixth sense of the seismic emotional pressure that exists in your home. Never underestimate the impact of words that can't be unsaid and actions that can't be undone.

What parents consider as acceptable behavior between siblings is key to the transition when they go out into the world. Home is where a child learns how to treat others. Often parents allow siblings to say hurtful things or to physically fight. Parents dismiss it with the caveat of kids will be kids. Some parents even believe allowing siblings to fight unfairly is somehow healthy. I can't emphasis enough that the opposite is true.

Bullying begins at home.

Bullies have been bullied long before they get to the playground or classroom. Give your children a place of safety and civility. You owe it to them. It's part of your job and responsibility as a parent.

Words can be worrisome, people complex, motives and manners unclear. Grant her the wisdom to choose her path right, free from unkindness and fear.
—Neil Gaiman, from *Blueberry Girl*

Within a few years, a child's social circle widens with interaction with friends and classmates. The scope of conflict increases as well when a child's behavior style conflicts with that of others. This is the beginning of understanding the currency of cooperation; one of the first basic coping skills.

As a parent or caregiver of a young child, there are key factors to consider for teaching age appropriate coping skills. I suggest questions that open a dialogue with a child that gives them their first awareness of their own feelings and the feelings of others. These are key factors in the development of childhood coping skills.

- Learning to stop and think about an undesirable reaction to conflict.

  Why are you angry?

  What does that feel like?

- Learning to think about and understand the concept of consequences.

  Was what happened what you wanted to happen?

  Is that why you did what you did?

- Learning to control negative impulses.

  Did you hurt anyone else (physically) by your actions?

  Did they hurt you (physically) in return?

  Did you hurt their feelings?

  What do you think that feels like?

  Do you like to feel that way?

  Would you want them to do that to you?

- Learning to make amends.

  How do you think they feel now?

  How can you make them feel better?

  Can you tell them you are sorry?

- Learning from mistakes.

  How do you feel now?

  Do you want this to happen again?

  What can you do the next time this problem happens?

These simple questions are instrumental in teaching a child to recognize the part they play in managing problems with analytical thinking. Better yet, understanding that some problems are avoidable is key. Then the practice of critical thinking becomes easier for making judgment calls as a child matures. This is the beginning of elementary citizenship where human values are established. It is also the groundwork of empathy.

These strategies can be effectively used as a response to bullying, in particular. Role-playing with structured scenarios can prepare a child for bullying before it happens. That awareness not only gives them the tools for coping but also identifies bullying as unacceptable behavior. This can be a catalyst for children to advocate for each other in bullying situations and foster support and encourage prevention.

Making and sustaining friendships fulfills a basic human need. Belonging is a necessary component for happiness. Most problems in childhood are rooted in finding a place in a community where there is acceptance and validation. The first community you inhabit is your family. Once you belong there, if you are fortunate, a confidence is instilled in you that validates you to your core. Then school, college, workplace, and other community experiences come naturally. If you don't receive that validation from the people who should be the most likely to accept you and love you, then you are at risk. You'll seek that acceptance where you can get it. That vulnerability opens the door for all sorts of jeopardy. That exposure leaves you more likely to allow yourself to be manipulated and controlled by someone who may not have your best interests at heart as long as you receive their attention.

It is vital that parents give this valuable emotional commodity to their children. Mothers set the standard for how women are treated. Your belief system about how men act is set by what your father demonstrates. Fathers of daughters are inextricably woven into the fabric of their daughter's self-esteem. If the first man in your life who should innately find you easy to love and irresistible to adore fails to give you that birthright, then you will spend the rest of your life searching for it in every man that comes along. A young son repeats the patterns he witnesses his mother receive from his father. He will mirror honor and respect or replay indignity and abuse.

Want to know how to raise great kids?

Be the person you want them to be.

Teenagers

Along the way from child to adult is that location in life that can feel like going through hell. They call it teenage angst for a reason. You wake up one day to find everything is different. Everything is changing without your permission. Your body, mind, and emotions seem to be working against you. Your parents aren't helping with the microscope they've put you under and the way they've magnified the problem. You've never felt so out of place. You're happy and you're sad.

It doesn't help that your friends are changing as well, and it's harder to know what to do or whom to trust. You've become old enough that you have a little more freedom. You're thrilled and you're scared. Now you find yourself facing more problems. You're conflicted and confused. Peer pressure, social media, parental expectations, school requirements, gender identity, sexual orientation, and self-confidence battle for your attention. All the possibilities and choices roll around in your head crashing into each other. Your mind hurts. Brain fog sets in and nothing is clear. Your dad's sports metaphors as advice and your mom's inspirational sticky notes on your mirror aren't cutting it. And they're irritating. Then they have the nerve to tell you these are the best years of your life. Are they kidding?

The key factors for facing these stressors and coping through them are a matter of perspective unique to the phase of life you're in right now. You're too old to get away with kid stuff and too young to be allowed to act like an adult.

It pretty much sucks.

You wish everyone would leave you alone and stop asking about what's going on. You aren't really sure what you want, except for this crappy feeling to stop. You feel totally out of control.

I want you to know this: You're more in charge than you think.

Ask yourself these questions about the problem situation and consider these strategies to help:

- Is the problem really an irritation that's got you ticked off? You can choose to opt out.

- Can you take a minute and stop before you act on any impulse or emotion you may feel? Sometimes a moment is all you need to decide what to do and to maybe avoid a problem before it blows up.

- Can the problem be avoided? You can adjust your attitude. Don't let it get under your skin and limit the impact.

- Does the problem require a decision that may cause a follow-up situation that you might not want to happen? This is that consequence thing your parents are always talking about.

- Will your decision affect other people?

- Would you want someone to involve you if they had the same problem?

- Look at the problem like it was happening to someone else. Be your own best friend and give yourself the advice you would give them. This will help take the emotion down a notch.

- Take a minute to breathe. Be still. Let your mind catch up.

You're braver than you give yourself credit for and more powerful than you think despite the messages you're getting. Think you're powerless? Feel like everyone else is in control of your life? I've got a great suggestion. Get more control in your life by taking the time to make smart decisions. Ask questions if you feel uneasy about someone or a situation. Listen to your inner voice. That sounds like woo-woo stuff, or something your mother would say, but it's for real. Use it. It's reminding you what your parents taught you, what you know from experience is right, and what your spirit knows is true.

You want more freedom and autonomy to make your own decisions. Earn it with good choices. You'll be amazed at the impact and power being trustworthy and responsible holds with your parents. It's real currency to barter for your freedom.

You *are* limited by your age in many ways, and by the parameters the adults in your life put in place. Some of those limits are going to be lifted only by time. You'll get older and they'll fall away. Other limits are negotiable with the currency of maturity. That can empower you and be disarming to a parent in a good way and open possibilities to freedoms. Make this work for you.

Surround yourself with a posse of friends who think like you, care about the same things as you, and, most importantly, value and respect you. Can't find a group to call your own? Even a single true, deep friendship can be enough.

Remember you get what you give. Choose the good stuff.

If you're reading this because you are the parent of a teenager, I beg you to remember what it was like to be in that awful place. You know it. You've been there to one degree or another. Even for the kids that appear popular or adjusted this is treacherous ground ever-shifting under their feet. The potential for emotional peril is always on high-alert. Consider every teen as high risk for emotional distress and you'll be much more prepared for any disruption to their well being. You don't have to be alarmed at that fact, be alert instead.

Have mercy.

Young Adults

Congratulations. You made it through the obstacle course of childhood, the pitfalls of adolescence, and the pressures of leaving home and becoming independent. A couple of decades of other people telling you what to do every minute of the day, and now they're asking what you're going to do next. In the same breath they're telling you what they think you should be doing. Don't buy into that. *They* take a backseat to you in your picture at this point. You get to decide where you go from here.

The trouble may be that you're not sure where you want to go. You're flying without a net. Now, there's no one waiting to catch you when you fall back. Being independent sounds great, but it's hard. You're bombarded with new problems. The solutions now involve career paths, coworkers, and future partners to be considered. You not only have to get a job, a relationship, and a grown-up life, but you have to find your purpose.

It's overwhelming.

It can be paralyzing.

Maybe you've made some life choices already, but now you're not sure if those were really the right ones for you. Let me tell you about Sean.

Sean was a young man who needed clarity on his career choice his senior year in college. Three generations of his family had built and operated a very esteemed and lucrative accounting firm. His place and his success were guaranteed. In addition, his father's heart was set on the dream of his son leading the fourth generation of the firm.

Sean's trajectory was perfect on paper. He was a math whiz, had great organizational skills, had been accepted to graduate school, and was focused on a goal. It had all gone according to plan.

Until his senior year.

With every math course offered under his belt, Sean found himself lacking the prerequisite number of electives to graduate. He settled on the only class that fit his packed schedule. It was glass blowing. He knew nothing about glass blowing and didn't want to know anything about it. The idea of it irritated him as a ridiculous waste of time. Graduate school, advanced accounting practices, and his future were dependent on one art class he had no interest in taking.

You might guess what happened. In that class he dreaded and wished he could avoid, Sean found his passion. Not only did he adore the creative process, he discovered that he was a gifted artist. You can imagine in his bliss of that discovery, he found himself conflicted and struggling with doubt, fear, and guilt. His entire family and especially his father, were set on him coming into the family firm and fulfilling that collective dream. Suddenly and unexpectedly, his perfect life plan became a burden. When he reached out for help, the agony of the decision he was facing had manifested in anxiety attacks and depression.

His initial thoughts were of regret that he had spent so much time and energy pursuing a career he might abandon. He was terrified of his father's reaction and his disappointment. Fear of making a mistake by choosing the wrong path overwhelmed him. He questioned his judgment and ruminated over whether this was a whim or a calling.

He opened himself to the realization that those kinds of choices can be viewed as conflicts or opportunities. That in no way discounted the discomfort and pain he was feeling, but supported and justified his decision either way. He had two great paths before him with a high degree of potential for success at both. Being good at two very different things could bring him satisfaction, or he could let the conflict of choosing between them cloud his vision. His biggest choice was whether or not to see the problem for the possibilities.

We worked together to examine the facts while Sean sorted through the emotions of each option and decided to follow his heart and pursue his passion. Within weeks the depression lifted. The anxiety he felt was situational and dissipated after he told his family his decision. Disappointing his family wasn't easy, but Sean knew he made the right choice for his happiness. It took time, but his father came around as the biggest fan of Sean's work as an artist. Sean's father also became his accountant.

At this mile marker on the road of your life, it's easy to get caught in traffic. It's like trying to drive in midtown Manhattan. You're in the flow, but how fast you can go is governed by lots of other drivers. You might not be able to make a turn or change lanes without someone else's cooperation. Sometimes there are unexpected construction detours that aren't registering on your car's GPS. Your destination is somewhere ahead, but you can't see it and have no way of knowing for sure if you'll get there going the way you've chosen.

Some people might find this exciting. You might find it incredibly frustrating. Or you can see it as not worth the hassle, so you've decided to opt out and stay put. The other drivers are yelling advice to you to do something, move on, watch out, or get off the road, while they voice their opinions about your choices and ask you the same question that you're asking yourself.

What the hell do you think you're doing?

You wish you knew.

So, let's start with these questions to clarify your position:

- Do you know where you want to go? If you have no idea don't worry. Many people don't know for sure at this point.

- Do you know where you *don't* want to go? Sometimes that's a great place to start. The more options you can delete from the list the closer you come to the best choice.

- Do you see multiple ways to go at this intersection or are you at a dead end?

- Do you have some ideas of where next might be for you?

- Have you done anything to test the waters of that new place to see if it feels good to you?

- What experiences have you had that you can stand on to give you a view to that place?

- Is there someone important in your life who feels like a roadblock?

- Are you the obstacle blocking your way forward?

- Will you take a risk on an unknown road to see where it leads or do you need the security of a set and certain path?

Mid-Life

Ok, I know being thirty isn't being middle aged, but it does usually mean being in the middle of establishing your adult life in terms of decisions about marriage, kids, and career. This is commitment time and the phase of life you spend all of your energy and a good portion of your income fulfilling the requirements those commitments demand.

Relationships require an enormous amount of energy. They're complicated and ever challenging, even when they work well. You learn to put someone else's needs before your own. Compromise, sacrifice, compliancy, generosity all become part of the vocabulary of being part of a couple. Then there is the option to not commit to one person exclusively. This is a huge decision that is part of the "you" that you envision. It also becomes a component in the way other people see you and treat you. We'll talk more about relationships in the next chapter.

Your career choices hold another set of commitment issues. Have you found your place in your career? Have you set up indecision as flexibility when its actually avoidance? Are you doing what you want to do or what others tell you that you should be doing?

Once you're in your forties, you may not feel like you're middle-aged. Middle means halfway through, and at forty you're halfway to eighty. Double fifty, and you're talking about living to be one hundred. This can work for you if you let it. Look at all you've done. You survived childhood. You made it through grade, middle, and high school and maybe college or graduate school.

You've been in love, been jilted a time or two, searched for the right person, found employment, made a home for yourself and maybe others. You probably got a dog. Or a cat. That's a lot of living. And you're only halfway through. Now look how much is still in front of you. There's plenty of time left and countless experiences waiting. It still may not be all you expected, or it might not be anything like you expected.

So, by the time you are in your mid-forties, you're middle-aged. You're probably also deep into your career. Are you feeling restless and curious if this is really where you are supposed to be in your work life? Maybe you're where you expected to be at this point, but it no longer excites you, or maybe it hasn't gone as well as you anticipated. This is where a great deal of anxiety presents in thoughts of "what now" and "is it too late" that bombard you until you are wracked with confusion. Then you become discontented and possibly depressed. That can lead to another form of paralysis.

My first go-round in college I majored in business. I would get a business degree as an obvious choice for someone dating a guy whose family business was going to be his vocation. What I really wanted to do was major in psychology. As far as my future mother-in-law was concerned, I might as well have said I wanted to be a pole dancer. She equated the usefulness of each as the same. (No offense on my part intended here. I support all sorts of career choices.) I was young and as eager as a needy lapdog to please her and everyone else.

Fast forward to years later. I returned to college at age thirty-seven to reboot my life. I reclaimed my destiny and declared psychology as my major. I lacked only one year to graduate on my original track and changing disciplines meant more prerequisite hours and more tuition that I had no idea where I would get. I went on faith, ignored the nays, including those in my own head, and listened to my gut.

The fear of change can immobilize you. You can't handle the uncertainty. Status quo feels safe and easy. Or maybe you're tired of thinking about it. The effort and all the disruption making a change would cause doesn't feel worth it. And then there's that issue of the other people in your life.

How will it affect your partner? Your kids?

Even reading about it on this page exhausts you.

Ok, deep breathe instead. Let's talk about a different way to look at being in the middle of mid-life.

- Does your work life work for you?

- What would make it work better?

- Would you choose your job again?

- Was this job choice yours alone, or were you influenced by what someone else wanted for your life?

- What would you do instead?

- Is that choice grounded in reality or is it a knee-jerk to the dissatisfaction you're feeling?

- Have you done due diligence to discern your options?

- What, if any, preparation is required to leave your current job and secure the new one?

- If a change of job isn't possible at this moment, what can you do to help your situation work better for you?

- Are there things you can do now in preparation for the time in the future when you will be positioned to make the change you desire?

- Is the change you seek really about what you are focusing on or something else altogether?

- Are finances part of your consideration? Are you limited in the short term due to finances? What could make the difference for your decision?

- Are you considering all the people in your life that are affected by your decisions?

- Is your consideration of them truly a factor of their well-being or are you afraid of what they will think?

- Are you motivated by a sense of your better judgement or the fear of being judged by others?

- Can you distinguish between rational thinking and rationalization to justify your feelings? For example, are you stuck because you're depressed or depressed because you are stuck? This important difference can free you to see things in a new and workable way.

- Are you cementing yourself in regret about things that haven't gone your way?

- Can you allow yourself to let those thoughts go so their hold on you is released?

Then there's the question of purpose that comes up. The problem may be that you don't find fulfillment in what you are doing. You feel guilty when you see someone else doing global good in noble ways or when their choices seem motivated by bliss rather than regard for monetary gain. There are the five-year-olds who are published authors spreading social messages to change the world, high schoolers establishing foundations for global outreach, and adults who ditch their careers and all of the coveted materialism dangling before us to help save endangered species in remote parts of the planet. It appears that everybody is passionate about something and following it into their bliss. It's a struggle to not be depressed if you don't feel like you stack up.

Then there's the unrelenting pressure to achieve emotional nirvana in a cocktail of bliss *and* wealth. *Find your passion, and the money will come.* How many times have you heard that? It is the mantra of CEOs and celebrities. You want to tell them you think that's easy for them to say sitting in their mega-mansion with the Bentley in the drive, but right now you're passionate about trying to pay your mortgage on time.

This is a problem particular to the modern world. Money is a scorecard. That's not a bad thing unless you allow it to define your worthiness, dictate your contentment, and determine your happiness. You're bombarded with constant reminders through social media, television, and the movies that foster continuous competitive measurement. It seems like everyone is out there living fabulous lives as a result of their passion. Instagram grinds you with each swipe as you shuffle the digital deck of magazine cover pictures of other people's homes, beach condos, lake houses, cars, boats, and vacations. Then it's the *everybody but you* syndrome. Kindergarteners on TikTok become influencers, preteens are getting recording contracts from YouTube postings, and everybody's an entrepreneur on Shark Tank. What's wrong with *you*?

What's your passion? What's your purpose? These have become mental wellness keywords. They also can feel like another burden on your already weary mind. You may not have time or the energy to think about metaphysical life questions. Your list of things to do and ways to stay on track is already too long to handle.

Let's look at it another way. First, let's establish that a hobby is not a passion. You might really, really love to play tennis, but you're not ever going to be striving for ranking at Wimbledon. You're a really fine home chef, but Gordan Ramsey has no need to think you are coming for his timeslot. Though both of these are viable careers for those who chose them as that, the reality is you can feel passionate about something you enjoy without it being the main focus of your life. There are the things you can be passionate about that will probably not be financially beneficial, but the measure of success comes from self-satisfaction.

So, what is a passion? How to identify *your* passion?

Sara Blakely the founder of SPANX says you should ask yourself what breaks your heart.

Wow. I think Sara nailed it.

But you're saying: Becki, I'm already heartsick. That sounds so sad and depressing. Passion is supposed to be the thing that gives your soul wings, right? Exactly. Passion is soul stuff.

What I take from Sara's mandate is that your passion is anything you care about so deeply that you would be heartbroken if you no longer had it in your life. This explains why some people pursue a career with a high rejection rate and never give up. Writers say they can't stop writing. Dancers sacrifice their bodies for little pay. Singers will play the small clubs for decades with no sign of hitting the big time because life without sharing their song, even if it's with only one other person, is unthinkable. Financial reward isn't the motivation. The *doing* is the motivation. The reward is being a part of something that you feel is a part of you. That connection is so inherently bonded, it is inseparable from your happiness.

If you work hard and pursue your passion with excellence, the popular adage of *the money will follow* may happen for you. You'll certainly find that true passion has a currency all its own. This is where bliss comes in. Also keep in mind that passion has no time limits. It's with you always and there whenever you decide you can no longer keep your distance.

It waits for you.

So, what's purpose? What's passion? Aren't they the same thing?

The idea of purpose and the idea of passion are talked about interchangeably. I don't believe they're the same.

Some people have a passion for something they love to do. The measurement of success with your passion has nothing to do with others' judgment of its worthiness but in the great joy it brings you in doing it. Purpose is your reason for being. It's your mission. It's your mandate. It's the worthy goal for your life. The important difference is your passion benefits *you* while your purpose benefits *others*. When you are truly blessed, your passion leads you to your purpose.

If all that weren't enough, mid-life is also the place where you come to a juncture in the road with two possible directions to choose from that will determine your path going forward in a major way. One road will lead to adding children to your life plan. For some people, happiness and fulfillment are not predicated on the idea of having children, so they choose the other.

Maybe you are struggling with this major life decision. Your friends are having babies. Your mother is begging to be a grandmother like all of her friends. Your father is pressuring you to carry on the family name. Your in-laws are wondering what's wrong with you and what's taking so long. Your grandmother is threatening to die unhappy if you don't grant her this wish to see her great-grandchildren born.

That's where Tory was when she told me her story. She had

never felt an inclination to be a mother. Her sisters had children and most of her friends did as well. She adored her nieces and nephews but knew that her life plan didn't include her own children. She was in a committed relationship with a great guy. He was on board with her decision and agreed they could have a full life just the two of them.

The problem was Tory's mom Shelia. She was heartbroken. She could not imagine her child would be childless. Whenever they were together, Shelia brought it up in every way possible from sarcastic comments, to admonishments, to accusing Tory's boyfriend of brainwashing her into the decision because he was the one who didn't want children.

Tory felt resentment and anger that her mother didn't understand but also felt guilt that she was disappointing her mother. When we talked, Tory examined her legacy and it became clear her mother Shelia's life mission had always been to be a mom. Her entire identity was dependent on being the perfect mother. Tory was able to see that the problem originated with her mother's point of view. Shelia believed that Tory's choice to not have a child was a negative reflection of Shelia's parenting. The workable solution was for Tory to stand confident in her decision for her life while making it clear to Shelia that it had nothing to do with her.

The burden was then on Shelia to accept and respect Tory's decision. Even if that didn't happen, Tory had to prepare herself to shed the unnecessary guilt. It wasn't hers to carry. Tory's mission was to put her resentment aside, thoughtfully appeal to her mother's ultimate desire to see Tory happy, and to help her understand not having children was Tory's chosen path. She assured Shelia that she was a wonderful mother and a hard act to follow.

Shelia realized her resistance hurt Tory. She felt disrespected when in actuality she was disrespectful of Tory's decision. The idea of that was far more painful than her imagined insult. Then the two of them began to focus on the children in their family that they both currently shared—Tory reveled in being the fun aunt, and Shelia focused on the grandchildren already in her life. Together they shared the joy of having that love in common.

If the problem in your life concerns the decision whether or not to have children, I urge you to give much thought to the permanence of parenthood. Once the decision is made to have a child and the nursery is perfectly decorated, a name is finally chosen, the baby shower is over, and the sweet one arrives, you will be a parent forever.

It is the most demanding commitment you will ever make.

You can do-over a spouse. Not so with a child.

You can't give them back when they become inconvenient.

You can't trade them in for another model.

You can't walk away and forget as if they never happened.

You are a parent until you die.

The beauty is you are a parent until you die. You are part of a bond with the reciprocal love and devotion of another human being who is forever part of you. It is part of the bargain you make.

If you chose not to become a parent, be confident that it was the right decision for you. You owe no explanation and no apologies for it.

Whether you choose to have no children or a dozen, that decision should never be up for judgment. If you find yourself in that position, defend it with your actions not reactions. You'll be an example of the right way it's done.

If you chose parenthood, be kind and respectful to those who don't.

Vice versa.

Like getting married, once you become a parent, you enter a phase of your life that is accompanied by specific problems that come with the territory of *it's not just about you* anymore.

It will never be just about you ever again. Ever.

Likewise, you're part of an extraordinary experiment in human behavior.

The problems don't go away as your children grow up, but the problems do change forms. Each age has its own difficulties and challenges. And joys.

A young child has a small viewpoint of the world. That world is the one their parents provide. You rule their universe. The reward is they believe you are the center of the universe. You may never feel this totally unabashedly loved again.

A teenager longs to create their own version of the world because living in this one by the adults' rules is so very difficult. A teen has only one giant set of responses regardless of the size of any problem. Everything is a big deal. Everything. They can't help it or explain it to you. More importantly, they can't explain it at all. You don't understand them. They don't understand themselves. It seems as though you're on opposing sides. The reality is you share a common confusion. Find the kinship in that. Use it as a starting place to commiserate and communicate. Mutual compassion is amazingly powerful common ground. Build a foundation on it together to make a strong and safe place for your teenager.

It's hard up until the teenage years and then you find yourself parenting a young adult.

Kids do grow up. You find yourself wandering through a relationship where you once reigned supreme. Now your child is an adult with all the privileges that entails. With the passing of a birthday, all of a sudden the two of you are legal equals, and you must transition from guardian and instructor to admiring fan. This is what they want from you now. This is what you must give them for their sake and yours.

What you want is for someone to explain to you how after twenty-one years of being the voice of authority, no one's listening. A freshly minted adult child no longer thinks you have all the answers.

In fact, they may believe you don't have any and they now possess the secret of life. Problems arise when your rules are overturned and your jurisdiction dissolves. This requires a major adjustment for everyone. The key is balance. You've invested your heart and soul with all of your intent in these people. Now you must find a happy place between that and letting them be who you have helped them become.

There are the other complicated parts of your life in the midlife location. There are mortgages to pay and cars to maintain, marriages and relationships to keep fresh, careers to keep on track, and your purpose to pursue. Responsibilities and obligations conflict with dreams and desires.

You've met the problems and challenges of life decisions about your vocation, partners, children, the paths you've taken, and the ones you've avoided. Now the problems facing you come in new forms with new consequences. Children become parents themselves and need you less. Your parents are aging and need you in new ways. The people you have spent a lifetime gaining independence from are now dependent on you. Decisions become time-sensitive. Looking back may hold regret and looking forward may be harder. You find youth and health are not givens going forward with both require adjustments in action and in attitude. Emotional arrows are slung at you from every direction.

This is when internal stressors come into play as well. Disappointment threatens to overtake the joy. The what ifs, should haves, and could haves become interpersonal enemies you battle. Depression and anxiety can prevail. Substance abuse and addiction may result and add to the list of problems. This is when self-care shifts from an option to a necessity. You must make a plan to manage problems of unexpected predicaments and unrealized expectations with careful intent. The upside here is you have a list of accomplishments to stand on to help you see past any difficulty. You've earned the respect of others and yourself. You've also put many moments of happiness in your memory bank account to call upon as measures of your success and as sources of joy.

Seniors

Next location on the life road after the rough mountainous terrain, the perilous steep curves, the sinkholes, and the lull of straight stretches of open highway and blue skies is altogether new landscape. If you check the sixty-five and older box, the problems you face are a different territory. If that's not your location, it probably is where you find your parents or grandparents.

At this mile marker, you've completed most of the requirements, accomplished much, and survived. Now the world wants to put you in another type of box that has little or nothing to do with who you envision you are. You may not look or feel old, but every type of media tells you otherwise. You want to be relevant in a world that no longer looks at you twice.

Then there's the fact that you've become a card-carrying member of a group you didn't choose. A social security card doesn't exactly have the same cache as obtaining American Express Centurion status, or even Gold.

It means you are now a health statistic waiting to happen.

Your contemporaries' conversations center around diseases, ailments, maladies, lab numbers, obituaries, and the possibility of replacing body parts with bionic pieces. Most things take more effort. Besides the physical, it's the emotional effort required to be heard rather than discounted, to be seen rather than being invisible, and to be considered instead of being overlooked.

It's jarring to your soul to think that time left is shorter than time spent. The irony is you now have more time in the day but less days left to count. Changes in living situations and your autonomy present unique problems and challenges. Sometimes the choices are no longer yours. Bereavement is unescapable as friends, loved ones, partners and family numbers dwindle. If you let it, loss will become an overriding theme.

Then there's the matter of what can fill your days now. Whether it's your work, children, spouse, or lifestyle, all have altered in some way and the time and attention they require has changed, often dramatically. Your identity may be in question in other people's minds and your own. You may feel your options are limited now. When you were young the choices were almost endless. Now your age limits them. It can be frustrating and, if you allow it, depressing. Many people slip into a slow undertow that drags them into decline. Only deliberate strokes can get you back to solid ground.

Consider these questions and possible choices:

- Are you doing everything you can to stay youthful? This is about your attitude. It doesn't mean plastic surgery or cosmetic procedures to keep age at bay. Those are viable options if you do it for you. But it shouldn't feel like forced compliance. However, the only way societal change happens is when one by one people think and dare to act in a new way. What if you stopped judging older women by their wrinkles and chose to accept them as part of their beauty? What if you stopped equating your worth with your reflection? What if you stopped being scared of aging? You could change the world.

- Do you want the young people in your life to talk about you or with you? Stay relevant. Don't give in to the stereotypes. Don't give up. It's easier to let your guard down, stop exercising, slack off on taking care of your appearance, or be afraid of technology, or worse yet, be afraid to learn. To keep your mind, sharpen it.

- Are you willing to resist humming the blues and get a new play-list? Choose a theme song so infectious that everyone around you can't help but listen and sing along. This can be literal or figurative. If you want people to want to be around you and not leave you out of their lives, attract them with your attitude.

- Feel like you don't fit into today's world? Find common ground and claim it. The young people in your life need what you have to offer. They don't feel like they fit either. You possess a richness of experiences and wisdom. They need your counsel. You can choose to give the people around you a reason to invite you to the table. Take your seat. You deserve it.

- When you face a senior wellness issue, whether it's physical or your mental health, will you seek and accept the help your loved ones offer? Allow them to partner with you to find workable solutions to make your life more comfortable.

- Can you consider the possibility that you can think yourself young again? Youthful isn't just an adjective, it's an attitude. It's curiosity, acceptance of change, and a willingness to make the effort. Boldness is an option at any age.

This location in life has many rewards to focus on and to build upon. Now your time is truly your own. You get to make choices from a more self-centered focus. You get to put you first.

You've determined your location, but chances are you're not traveling alone. You have other people in the sphere of your life that you connect with to some degree. Let's talk about what gives you the most satisfaction and joy and is the source of much of the difficulty in your life—your relationships.

CHAPTER FOUR:

YOUR RELATIONSHIPS

The three components in the previous chapters are key to the kinds of relationships you have in your life. This is why it's so important to examine them. Your legacy serves as the template of how you believe relationships work: The ways you fight, make amends, create expectations of how much the other person in the relationship gives or takes, and lay the ground rules for acceptable behavior are set there. Your wiring sets the tone for how you function within your relationships and how your emotions affect your responses. Your experiences are huge factors in whether you continue to repeat patterns. Those experiences and your location on your life road more than likely dictate that there are other people to be considered as part of your landscape or as collateral damage if you careen into a ditch.

Because you live in this world, you have relationships. Because you have relationships, and people have differences, you have problems. You may immediately think in terms of relationship status like your social media profile. That may be listed as single, but you have other relationships or at least interactions as you encounter dozens of people in your everyday life. Picture an imaginary circle around you. Let's look at that.

The Periphery

When you think of drawing a circle around you and the people in your life, you probably think in terms of your family and best friends. At its widest, your circle actually includes the most casual of your relationships. You might not have thought about them in that way. You interact on a regular basis in your daily life with lots of people that aren't your family or closest friends.

There are people in your life who are part of it because they are store owners or sales associates where you shop, they manage and provide services you use, they park next to you in the garage at work, they're your neighbor, or they're your child's teacher. They are all part of your relationship circle. How you connect with those people is important. Any relationship, no matter the emotional or time investment, is a possible problem source. Again, this isn't to depress you. It's to prepare you so that you can problem solve and handle the stress in the best possible way.

Strife that originates with another person comes in varying degrees. It can be a mere annoyance, or an uncomfortable situation involving a personality clash, conflicting communication style, or lifestyle issue. It may even be philosophical or ideological in nature. That might sound broad, but you live in a world with people who differ from you in many ways. That provides an automatic setup for conflict between differences of opinion and viewpoints. You may have an unpleasant relationship that eats away at your contentment. If the relationship that's causing you difficulty is one that is on the farthest outside of your circle, let me ask you:

- How integral is this relationship to your everyday life? Would it be disruptive to you if it was no longer a part of your life?

- How important is this relationship to you? Consider if you have even the smallest of emotional connection to the person. Would it be undesirable to stop the relationship?

- Can you make a change that would alleviate or eliminate the problem? This could be something logistical, or it could be a change in the way you approach the problem.

- Are you willing to make the change?

- Does the way you behave in the difficult relationship affect ones closer to you?

- Are you willing to let go of the problem altogether? Take the drama out.

Now, pull that view of the circle around you closer in. Who do you see here? These relationships are the ones that become part of your life by association. Because they are part of the life of someone or something you choose to have in yours. You accept a job and you get co-workers. Your child has friends and they have parents. Your friends have friends. Your partner has a family. Your partner has friends. They all come with the territory. The person closest to you in this association is the primary relationship in these situations. Let's talk about what you can do about a problem that may be troublesome in this category.

- How important is the primary relationship to you? This can be a practical relationship like with a boss or a deeper love relationship. This refers to the emotional investment of the relationship. Does it matter to you on a heart level? This means that it matters to you that it be workable and mutually beneficial.

- Is the person you care about in the primary relationship aware of the problem? Sometimes the person isn't tuned in to the fact that someone else in their life is the source of discomfort to you.

- How does the primary person feel about the fact that someone they have brought into the circle is a problem source?

- What is the primary person willing to do to help the situation?

- What are you willing to do to make concessions for a compromise?

- Are you clear on your boundaries?

- Is the primary person aware that you have those boundaries?

- Is the discord worth the damage to the primary relationship? Consider their feelings and their position. They're in the middle of a problem between two people in their life. They may or may not share your need for cooperation.

- Is it important to you to have harmony all the way around or can you separate your feelings from the primary person you care about and the other person who is the problem source?

Your Family Circle

Now, let's talk about the circle as it moves closer to you. Your family is that part of you that is forever determined. You can detach, but you never change that innate connection. The more you can do to gain insight into who they are as individuals by looking at their perspectives will only benefit you as you seek contentment. You've examined the factors we've talked about in your life; now look at theirs. Think of the role of their legacy, their wiring, their experiences, their relationships in terms of their hopes and dreams and their disappointments as well.

Your siblings are your first introduction to collaborative relationships. Beyond the issues of rivalry and jealousy there is a bond that comes from a shared environment. A tribe-like loyalty comes from a sense of cooperation. Others bond as soldiers on the same battlefield. In the same way you have changed over time, your siblings have been altered by their experiences. You grew up together and now you have the opportunity to grow together as adults. You will need each other as time goes on and family responsibilities shift generations. Here are some things to consider:

- How would you define your current relationship with your sibling?

- Are you willing to see your sibling, not as the child they were, but as the adult they have become?

- How did your parents treat your sibling?

- Were they correct in their behavior?

- How did your parents' opinions about your siblings shape yours?

- Are you willing to acknowledge your sibling's relationship with your parents, looking back on it with your maturity to see it not from a rivalry standpoint, but with understanding of the complexities that always exist between each child and parent?

- Can you separate and reconcile the differences that may have existed between how your parents treated your sibling in contrast to how they treated you?

- Are you willing to let that be in the past and move forward from it?

- Do you have empathy for the things in your sibling's life that may have been difficulties?

- Have you offered your emotional support in those times?

- Has your sibling been there for you?

- Was that their choice or yours?

- Do you want to make amends in the relationship?

- Are you doing anything to hinder cooperation with your sibling?

- Are you doing anything to encourage cooperation?

- Are they receptive to your efforts?

- If the relationship is at a stalemate, do you have a plan in place for establishing cooperation between you and your siblings at a future date where your parents are concerned?

Whether you are close or have grown apart, there will be a time that you may have to come together again with your siblings as decisions are made for your parents' changing needs. Their living situation, caretaking, and financial concerns will become your concerns as well to some degree. More than likely there'll be a dynamic shift and role reversal. This is difficult at best. You need all the allies and reinforcements you can gather. You may also encounter the most resistance you can imagine. First it will be from your aging parent, which is to be expected. What you might not expect is reluctance from your siblings. They may not participate as you would like. They may refuse to support your efforts. I have seen countless situations where this is the case.

In this place in your life there are many questions to consider when problems arise about aging parents.

- Have you and your siblings discussed what the inevitable course that caring for your aging parents entails?

- Are you all on the same page and committed to being on board?

- Have you discussed with your parents their concerns, fears, and wishes for their later life?

- Have you agreed on and designated a leader in the process? I refer to this person as the COO, Chief Operating Officer of the family firm. They serve as the spokesperson, go-to, tiebreaker, and final say of the group if you have siblings. If you don't have siblings, then are you prepared to be the decision maker?

- If both parents are living, do you have a plan in place for either of them to be the COO if the other becomes unable to make decisions?

- Are you and your siblings clear on that?

- Are you prepared to look past the logistics and the practical matters at hand and stay vigilant to your parents' emotional needs? It may be beneficial to separate these needs and assign the roles. One sibling may be better with the financial and practical matters and another is the emotional advocate. The chance to let each use their best skills will facilitate cooperation and prevent burnout on any one individual.

- Will you see this as a stellar opportunity to heal all sorts of familial pain? These considerations offer up those last chances to heal one-on-one with loved ones. It may be beneficial to remember you will be in this same location on your life road looking to your children to care for you.

Your Children

If you are a parent, this next section is for you. If you aren't, but you have someone important to you in your life who is, then you may want to read on to gain some understanding of what they are experiencing.

Your relationship circle gets tighter when it comes to making a family that you choose. Often this means adding brand-new humans to your picture who are totally reliant on you in every possible way. It is a commitment you can't break, one you can never undo no matter the time or distance that comes later.

Instructions Not Included

Remember when you saw your baby for the first time? The wonder of a totally new human with their entire life ahead of them felt so full of promise. You had a dream of what they would become and how they would fit into this world and make their way as a person of integrity, principle, and honor.

Now recall the huge sense of responsibility that came upon you in that moment when you realized you were and are still their north star. You're the most influential person in their life. You chose a road to travel the moment you became a parent and burned the bridge behind you that led to life before.

There's no turning back.

The requirements of being a parent are highly specialized and non-negotiable. Even though many are physically capable of creating children, not all are emotionally fully equipped or willing to do what is mandated. From the first moment a child enters your life you're asked to be of great physical stamina, good humor, have a strong constitution under pressure, be forever resilient, compassionate, tireless, clairvoyant, sympathetic, resourceful, creative, merciful, generous, selfless, and enthusiastic in the face of what feels like under-appreciation. And that's for a helpless infant.

Then you become a ninja of safety to rescue a toddler from all things that can be swallowed and infinite possible sources of falls and injury, a guardian of preschool hearts, a preceptor of grade school knowledge, and a sculptor of middle school citizens.

Then you're required to morph into a shapeshifter and become a covert operative sort of narc on patrol in anticipation of every possible misstep a teenager can make that holds the potential to bring it all thundering down in a moment of faulty judgment from a still-growing brain.

It's non-stop exhaustion.

It's built on pure joy.

Days are eternal and years are too swift. When it's tough and thankless, remember how essential you are to their care. You get one shot at being the parent they need. You must aim high.

This is where much of what you carry from your family legacy comes into play. You can repeat unsuccessful patterns, or you can implement change. You have a chance to fill in what wasn't there for you and provide it for your child.

You hear it said all of the time. You've probably said it yourself. There's no handbook for raising children. They don't come with instructions. But wisdom is all around you. More importantly, it is in you. You know what it's like to be a child. You know what the adults did in your life, and what of that worked and what you would have changed. Now's your chance to do it right. Having children invites problems into your life simply because it has so many moving parts and variables. I have a wonderful friend Margaret who recounts her father's rule of thumb for making parental decisions. What are the variables? I take that to mean look at the possible outcomes before you say yes to any request from your child. Careful consideration is your best defense and offense. My motto is: If you do all things from a place of love and honor, you can't possibly go too far off track.

> *What you do to your children matters. And they might never forget.*
> —Toni Morrison

For the problems that come with parenting, begin with what works for everyone. For small children, be patient and consistent. Consistency is *everything*. Consistency equals trust. You learn to trust what you know. Here's some things to check for consistency with bringing up children:

- Are your expectations clear? Make sure they understand in age-appropriate words. This is where taking the time to explain rather than dictate is one of the most important things you can do for a child. This is how kids learn to reason. That ability to reason is analytical thinking. Even small children can relate to this kind of cause and effect as consequences are made clear and follow-through is consistent. It's also the way a child develops what we call common sense.

- Are you adapting your expectations to be age-appropriate? It's important to give obtainable goals to promote compliance and success. Giving a child a realistic aim and a clear path to achievement increases their self-esteem. Setting a child up for an impossible task invites a sense of inadequacy and stifles initiative. This is the beginning of the fear of failure.

- Do you apply the same expectations to each child in the same way? Of course, this is dependent on age as well in some situations. You can't expect a toddler to have the same ability to reason as a first grader. If your expectations are inequitable, kids will notice. Siblings are like espionage moles. They see all. Nothing you do escapes their attention. They'll use all intel they gather against each other and you.

- Do you reinforce expectations with rewards and consequences?

Don't forget that meeting expectations deserves the reward of your attention as much as negative behavior deserves the consequences you put in place.

- Do you follow through every time and deliver what you declare? Consistency, consistency, consistency is the key to parenting. Follow-through is essential for praise and punishment. Praise should be conditional to behavior. Love must be ever-present.

- Do you hold yourself and your behavior to the same standards? One of my mantras for parenting is *Be the person you want your child to be*. They're watching.

- If you have more than one child, do you expect them to be alike? Children aren't clones. They may look alike, but they aren't the same in every way. Sometimes they aren't the same in any way. Let them be individuals. Recognize their differences and adapt to each of their needs rather than using a one-size-fits-all as standard measure. What works well for one usually doesn't work with the others. Bob and weave, zigzag, go with the ebb and flow or whatever dance you need to choreograph, but remember each has their own style. Adapt yours to theirs when needed.

- Do you have a clear and established threshold of trust? Young children will trust you because you are the most important person in their life. They will continue to trust you until you give them reason not to.

- Do you insist on respect from your child? This is more than politeness and manners. This is a core response to responsibility and fosters integrity.

- Are you deserving of their respect? Your small child is your biggest fan. Do not underestimate their devotion. Don't discount the idea that they will emulate you in every way. You are the first arbiter of what they believe to be worthy.

- Do you give them your respect as well? They may be small but they deserve the same consideration as any human. Only through reciprocation can concepts like respect be fully realized. A child's world is literally show and tell the first few years. Show them by example and tell them the truth.

Parenting Your Teen

For parenting teens, your role becomes a bit less instructional and a lot more transactional. You want them to do well in school, stay off of drugs, not have unsafe sex, keep out of trouble, not give you grief, make you proud, be compliant, be polite, and be a reflection of your values. That's all, right? But that's a pretty tall order if you think about it, especially if you're a kid and already overwhelmed by this growing up stuff. The problems in this part of your life and theirs are precarious and some hold perilous potential. You want absolute authority. They want freedom. It's a constant struggle to some degree.

You don't have the luxury of giving up.

Meet your teenager's emotional needs as you met their physical needs when they were fragile newborns. Never relinquish the care of their existence in your life. The Band-Aids they require at this age are the invisible kind but required for healing just the same. You can't spare them the pain of living in the world, but you can offer them the shelter of your love and acceptance.

You may remember being a teenager and your own adolescent angst, but for the same reasons your parents didn't understand what you were going through, you don't know the very specific territory of being a teen now. How do you continue to make sure they become those shiny happy people you imagined? It begins with an unbreakable, immovable commitment to be the best example you can be for them. Here are some questions to ask yourself about raising your teen and strategies to guide you:

- Do they have your attention? It may appear they aren't engaged, but they are acutely aware if you are tuned in to them or not.

- Do they have your time? This is your scarcest commodity. You're spinning plates and juggling balls in the air 24/7. They see how busy you are, so they know the value of the amount you devote to them. It's coveted validation.

- Are you actively listening to what they are saying? A teenager has a sixth sense about your authenticity.

- Can you listen harder for what isn't being said? Teens talk in riddles where their emotions are concerned. Rarely do they say what they mean and mean what they say. "I hate you" can mean "I'm frustrated that you don't have the answer." "Nobody likes me" can mean "I don't feel comfortable in my own skin."

- Are you making the effort to see their point of view? You have the brain development and the perspective from life experiences to know what your teenager can't possibly know yet. You have that advantage. Use it wisely and don't use it against them. Don't discount where they are on their life road. A little mercy goes a long way.

- Are you voicing judgment? Again, I remind you that you have the vantage point of having survived the teenage years. They aren't so sure they'll make it. You have the advantage of knowing looking back on this age won't be as hard as going through it. Be kind. Also remember that your words have penetrating abilities to sear right through a teenager's protective bravado to their soul. Your words leave an indelible imprint wherever they land.

- Do you expect respect from your teen?

- Is your teen clear that respect is always your expectation?

- Do you give them your respect as well? Reciprocity is the conduit of respect.

- Do you have a clear and established threshold of trust? Teenagers think in absolutes. Leave no room for confusion. They have enough confusion in their brains.

- Does that threshold apply both ways? Teenagers are limit testers, line in the sand crossers, and *just watch me* is their motto of resistance. They live in an unfair world and judge everything by that lack of fairness factor. If they think your rules don't apply to you, they aren't likely to comply with you. It diminishes your authority. And that authority, my friend, is gold.

- Do you have consequences for breaking the boundary of trust in place? Clear consequences should be your mantra and your mandate.

- Do you follow through? This is that consistency factor that began when your child was a baby. Trust is born from consistency. Trust is a matter of honor and it applies to being able to count on its presence. Your teen needs to know they can count on being in trouble if they break your trust. Sometimes it's what saves them when they can't think clearly enough to save themselves.

- If the trust is broken, do you offer a way for it to be earned again? Redemption is a sacred thing. Everyone needs to feel they can recover and rebound after a mistake. It is crucial for teenagers to know the offer and the power of forgiveness. Only then can they apply it to others. It's vital that they learn to bestow forgiveness to themselves as well. Remember that all of their emotions are super-sized. Their guilt and disappointment have profound impact.

- Does your teen know without a doubt that your trust can be withdrawn, but your love for them remains constant? Teenagers have short memories. They need specific reminders that your love is constant, but your approval is dependent on compliance. This goes a long way to establishing a sense of accountability that they will need out in the world and in their interpersonal relationships.

Parenting an Adult

And along the way your kids bring all sorts of individuals with them into their lives and yours that become part of the equation. There will be boyfriends and girlfriends to meet. Some you'll have the opportunity to get to know and love. Others you'll get to know, and you'll disapprove. Be prepared for the chance that you may begin to feel affection for someone who comes into your young adult child's life and decide that they are the perfect fit for your family only to have your child decide they aren't in love with them after all. I've worked with several parents who find themselves heartbroken after a relationship their child was having is over. They find that they had vested themselves in the idea of the relationship being permanent and view the breakup as a personal disappointment that the future they envisioned of that person being a part of their family is over. The disappointment often causes division and resentment between a parent and the adult child. You're called on to honor and respect your young adult child's choices, not choose for them.

Conversely, you may have to accept your adult child's decision to make a life with someone you don't think is right for them at all. This is really hard. Keep your comments as non-judgmental as possible. It's their choice, and they need your acceptance not admonishment. This is where future harmony lives. If the relationship between them lasts, your child won't hold the bad things you might have said about their partner against you. On the other hand, if the relationship doesn't last you will not be tempted to add insult to injury with, *I told you so.*

Then there are the other life decisions that these marvelous creatures you have molded and protected and cared for with every fiber of your being will make that will affect your life. You've spent their lifetime telling them what to do. It was your job. Now you're expected to back away and be silent. That's a very hard thing to do. It's like being forced from your job of decades into retirement.

You'll be asked to bite your tongue, hold your peace, eat your words, swallow your pride, and admit your mistakes. You'll also be astounded, wowed, blown away, and feel more gratitude than you could have ever imagined. You've asked them to be good people. Now, you must allow them the opportunity to show you what they learned. Your expectations up until this point have been mostly about their behavior. Now it's about you accepting their chosen lifestyle. That means letting go of your ideas of what that looks like. To ensure the best outcome, ask yourself these questions about your young adult children:

- What preconceived ideas do you have about who your children are and who they will become as adults? Examine where those ideas originated.

- How do you picture their future choices? Ask yourself if that has more to do with what you want than based on their personality, abilities, and desires.

- How will you react to anything they choose that does not match your mental picture? Take a moment to decide which is more important for the harmony of your relationship with your adult child: your dreams or theirs.

- Will you allow them the freedom to bloom their way? Putting parameters on your acceptance of their definition of happiness and success is the opposite of unconditional love.

- Will you listen more and tell less? Your adult child craves worthiness. Taking time to hear what they say before you offer advice or suggestions is one of the greatest forms of validation. It says you trust their ability to make decisions for themselves. It instills confidence to listen to your child, adult to adult. It is also another way to demonstrate mutual respect and foster cooperation.

- If your adult child does something or choses someone to be a part of their life that you feel is unacceptable, ask yourself why you believe that choice is unfavorable. Make sure your lack of support for the situation isn't just your opinion. If it truly is a matter of a problem that will cause them harm or they are behaving in a way that is detrimental to their successful functioning, then you should be supportive with your concerns and actions if needed. You never stop being their parent even when your parenting duties lessen.

When Your Children Have Children

The chances are you will be a grandparent if you have children. This is a category of life road location all by itself. The dynamics of stepping aside to allow your child to fill this role are complex. You've raised a child. You know this rodeo. You've lived it. But that was *your* rodeo. You haven't lived this particular one. This time you are an avid spectator. If you're fortunate, you get invited to be an active guest participant.

You wake up one day and your world has been changed in a colossal way by someone else. Chances are you're thrilled. You've waited for this phase of your life only to find out that grandparents get a bad and often undeserved rap. They're stereotyped as pushovers for all things parent forbidden and viewed as too stubborn to honor the wishes of the adorable child's parents. Grandparents are often viewed as frustrating in their non-compliance and comical in their resistance to change.

Some are.

Many are not.

"Grandparent" is a defining life label you receive without your permission or direct involvement. This sets up what I call a dynamic of degrees of participation some of which you choose and some is not yours to decide. You find yourself along for the ride. You aren't the driver. It's sort of like when you were teaching your teenager how to drive, and you covered your fear with a forced smile while they asked you to stop clutching the door handle or slamming an imaginary brake on the passenger side. It's often white-knuckle time while you let someone else take the wheel.

The challenges of relating to your child once they're a parent are tricky. Problems arise when they make choices for your grandchild that you don't agree with or are incongruent with how you raised your child. You believe there's one right way to parent. Now you're told there's *your* way and *their* way of parenting. Your wisdom may be met with opposition by a pronouncement of your method as old-school. Every generation of new parents seems to have a more prevailing concept of how to practice this ages-old ritual and rightly so. Times change. You don't disregard innovation or progress in other areas of your life why should you get stuck here? Be open.

Issues of territory and prevailing authority are best met with those all-important tools of respect, empathy, and compromise. You're wise to remember that now you have to work with not only your adult child on these issues, but an adult in-law child as well. They come into the situation with their own set of beliefs and practices from their childhood. That also means they're bringing their family legacy and another set of grandparents into your grandparenting world. Your vote isn't the only one. You may have to get in line to cast it. Your adult child and their partner will determine the order of succession so to speak. They will decide the strength of your position and involvement. You can enhance your position with understanding and patience.

The new little life that comes into yours may be tiny, but the cavern they carve in your heart and soul is gargantuan. They are your grandbaby. Yes, but you must share them.

The thing to remember is that baby's brand new parent is still your child. In your heart, they're not far removed from the newborn you welcomed all those years ago in the newness of your own parenting journey. You made promises to them then and they still hold. It's hard to watch someone you love struggle and harder to stay silent when they make a mistake. You desperately want to help. You want to make it better, easier when you can. Then there's that little one involved who holds your heart in their tiny hands. It's a delicate dance to be sure. Consider these questions:

- Can you be supportive not only in what you say about your child's parenting but with your silence? The most innocent comment can crush your child's confidence as a new parent. That continues throughout your grandchild's life. Your child will face challenges while raising your grandchild that you have already experienced and then some. You can throw rocks of blame or be the touchstone for family strength.

- Are you prepared to back away from any power struggle between your grandchild's parents? You will come to discover the differences in the two families of origin for each parent. You thought the wedding made that clear. You're about to find out more ways your families differ than you imagined.

- How about any conflict between you and the parents? Your relationship is directly affected by your biological relationship as the maternal or paternal grandparent and by the strength of your relationship to your child or their partner. This is the imperative for learning to get along with your child's partner before children enter the picture. If a bridge is built in the beginning, it will be there when you need it to cross this road.

- Are you willing to pick your battles? There may come a time when you feel so strongly that something your child is doing as a parent is detrimental to your grandchild that you must intervene. If you are argumentative or critical over lots of everyday issues, then when a real concern arises you have forfeited your parental clout and your grandparent privilege. It's easier to get through if you keep the path clear of unnecessary obstacles. You can create a blessing or a battlefield.

- Do you see your parenting job as done once your children have children? The opposite is true. Your children will need your help. At some juncture they'll realize they need it. They will probably need you physically to lend a hand and help out with the caretaking duties. They will always need you spiritually to be a cheerleader and an advocate for them as they make their way as parents.

Your Love Relationships

You may not think of yourself as a gambler. Think again. If you've ever been in love, you've hedged a huge bet. Love and intimacy are high-risk ventures. The exposure levels are high. You open yourself to personal loss and emotional injury while blinded by the dreams and possibilities of hitting the jackpot. If or when it doesn't pay off, you do it again. And again. And again. You can't resist the lure of the idea of the ideal relationship. All of the components we've discussed of family legacy, your wiring, phases of life location, and experiences determine your definition of ideal. That ideal may never waver over your lifetime. It may change and morph and transform with your experiences. It may be bolstered by early success. It may be battered and bruised along the way and hang on by a thread until you find what you desire. This may be the problem you are facing.

One of the most prudent and beneficial things you can do to ensure your ideal love relationship is to clear out all the clutter in your mind about what should be or can't be or won't be or will be for you. That will make room for the truth and the possibilities.

Clear your head to clear your heart.

Then you'll have full benefit of both.

Let's talk about that. You may be in a love relationship now. You may be thinking about one to come. You may be recovering from one that has ended. You may be trying to decide which of those applies to the problem you are dealing with by reading this book. Which ever scenario describes your situation, ask yourself these questions. If you are in a relationship be honest with yourself in your answers. If you have recently gone through a breakup, look at these questions to get clarity on what may have been the difficulty in maintaining that relationship and more importantly use them as guidelines for criteria to establish what you want in the next and best relationship in your life.

- What does the love of your life look like? I don't mean the physical description of the person. I'm asking about how your life with someone you love looks in your ideal scenario.

- Is it a movie version or more reality based?

- Does the relationship resemble your ideal?

- What do *you* look like in that relationship?

- Do you like what you see?

- If someone else described you in this relationship, would you recognize yourself?

- What about your relationship do you love most?

- What would you change?

- Is it something that has happened in other relationships before?

- Do you see a pattern you wish weren't there?

- Does your relationship work for you?

- Do you find yourself working hard at making it work?

- Do you think it should be that hard?

- Is there room for personal growth for you within the relationship?

- Is there room for personal growth for your partner in the relationship?

- Does your relationship foster a sense of belonging that excludes possession and ownership?

- Do you feel safe physically and emotionally in this relationship with this partner?

- Are you clear within yourself on what is acceptable and what is unacceptable in the way your relationship functions?

- Does your partner have a clear understanding of your tolerance levels?

- Do you have personal boundaries in place?

- Do you give in this relationship without giving up your personal identity?

- Do you have deal-breakers that you use as standards of behavior from your partner?

- Are you clear and consistent with identifying those deal-breakers to yourself?

- Is your partner clear on what your deal-breakers are?

- Do those deal-breakers have real consequences you are willing to enforce?

- Does your partner clearly understand those consequences?

- Are you willing to defend your standards without exception?

- What is your negotiation style for conflict and dispute resolution?

- What's your partner's disagreement/fighting style?

- Are you both agreed on clear rules of engagement in hashing out differences?

- Do you have a plan for redemption if trust is broken?

- Would you be friends with your partner even if you weren't in a love relationship? One of the crucial ingredients for a balanced and happy love relationship is a deep and abiding friendship. Got your back, go to the wall, do or die friendship that you give and expect so readily in a non-romantic relationship should be there in your love relationship as well. There will be times your romantic relationship will take a backseat to your life experiences. The sex will cool, the attraction will fade a bit, the affection will wane. These will revive and even roar back at different phases, but they are subject to all the other life issues that command your attention. The friendship will carry you when all else falls away.

We've talked about the factors that make you who you are and how they shape how you view a problem. So now let's talk about the problem that's brought us together.

CHAPTER FIVE:

YOUR WORDS MATTER

I've asked you to tell me about you. Now, tell me about the problem that's troubling you. To do that, you'll choose words to describe the place where you are, the people involved, and the feelings that accompany the situation. Sometimes doing that is easy because you have so much to say. Other times you can't begin to describe it because you can't quite identify what it is that's bothering you. If the latter is the case, that's okay because we'll talk it through.

You might want to literally talk it out. Do it out loud as you read if you like.

Then in as many or as few words as you feel ready to write, put them on paper. They can be in the form of a story or a journal entry. Scribble them in the margins of this book. It can simply be a list, but physically put down the words that describe the problem and the feelings you're having about it. Then place what you've written aside for now. We'll refer back to it a bit later.

You might be used to writing this sort of thing. I encourage journaling if it puts you closer to the feelings you need to express. This can be a great exercise for clarity in any situation. It often takes a while to come up with the right words. Those moments of consideration give you a time-out between your head and your hand to gather the emotions into a cohesive idea. That's why some therapists ask a client to write a letter about the difficulty. It may a letter to the person who has hurt you or abused you. It can be a letter to someone who has abandoned you in life or by death. Writing to your younger self can be a therapeutic method for understanding your emotions. Gratitude journals are very helpful to some people to stay on track to everyday mindfulness. If these help you, do them.

If you don't care for journaling, that's okay too. It isn't a prerequisite for mental and emotional wellness, only one of many tools. The last thing I want is for you to feel overwhelmed with one more "to-do" on your list. You're busy. You're tired. I get it. I also get the idea that you might be uncomfortable writing something down because someone might read it without your permission. It's a matter of intimacy and proximity to the raw feelings. Sometimes it's hard enough to look at your own thoughts staring back at you on a page, but the idea that someone else could read them is terrifying. It may feel like exposure you aren't willing to risk. So try saying it out loud if you like, or have this conversation in your head. It's your call.

Why does this matter to you right now? Because words are one of the most powerful and dynamic tools at your disposal. You can use them to advocate for yourself or others.

You can use them against yourself or others.

> *The best word shakers were the ones who understood the true power of words. They were the ones who could climb the highest.*
> —Markus Zusak

Words are amazing in their bounty and exquisitely effective whether used for good or for harm. They can empower and they can impede. They can wage war or make peace, wound or heal, clarify or confuse, delight or devastate, build or destroy, reward or punish, obscure or reveal, enlighten or mislead. When you speak or write, the words you choose are at your whim. You have the ability to bestow them with power and wield them at your will. Once you have released them, they can't be retracted completely. You can soften the blow or even change their shape with persuasion, but some residual effect remains. Spoken words may dissipate into the air, but their existence isn't voided. They leave an indelible emotional mark behind wherever they land. Remember to aim carefully.

Words are sacred if you honor their meaning.

Take the word *control* as an example. Control gets a bad rap. You want a pilot to be in control of the airplane you are traveling on, right? You control the temperature when you shower. You take control of the radio when you drive. But often when you hear the word control, you probably think in terms of limiting choices, domination, or restraining. Being in control doesn't mean being a control freak. That's an extreme form. A control freak wants to manipulate everyone and everything to satiate a power need that may have nothing to do with the situation and everything to do with their ego.

Being in control means taking the initiative. If no one is addressing a problem effectively, then someone has to step up and take charge if something constructive is going to get done. In the case of a problem, it's a matter of taking steps toward a resolution for a greater good for one or for many. We can't all be bystanders. That's when a leader is needed who takes command and responsibility. They opt in and do what's needed. If you're willing to take charge of a situation you believe requires that, then do it.

You may not want to step up. You might be willing to let others lead more often. However, when faced with a problem that is directly affecting your life, chances are you want to be the one moving the problem. That way you pick the direction. You want a voice in what happens to you. I urge you to reframe your idea of control to be a desirable one of personal power. If thinking about control is uncomfortable then think of taking charge. It's the place of peace you're seeking. A place where you decide what happens next.

Isn't that where you really want to be right now? The one calling the shots. The one who gets the final say. The one who decides the next step instead of waiting for the other shoe to drop. If you want to be sure to get where you want to go, and on your schedule, you need to be the one driving. Then the route and the pace are yours.

Likewise, self-control means taking responsibility for your choices. Be ready to stand by your actions.

Judgment is another maligned word. Saying you're passing judgment has an entirely different meaning than saying you're exercising good judgment. Same word but very different intent. We all are required to make judgment calls every day all day. Should you speed to get to work on time? Should you quit smoking? Do you let that person in traffic merge in front of you, even if they're being a jerk, or should you risk road rage? Do you tell your child it's okay to remain silent if the checkout person accidentally doesn't charge you for something, but then punish that child if they cheat on an exam for a higher grade? Do you buy that five-hundred-dollar pair of shoes that will blow your budget? Do you drink and drive? Do you let that co-worker's flattering attention go further and risk your marriage?

Using your better judgment is a clarion call for good. It is an optimum coping skill in life. Someone has to stand up and be accountable. Being judgmental in a way that demeans, disparages, or degrades anyone or any honorable thing is never favorable.

Another word that has a negative connotation is *denial.* This one's loaded. Like all words, the intent is affected by the context in which it is used. Denying reality can of course be very detrimental. If it interferes with life functioning, or if it is harmful to others in any way, then it is undoubtedly something to be recognized and addressed. Avoidance is a form of denial that can have destructive effects. Not dealing with a problem doesn't make it go away and many times inaction will actually make the problem worse. Facing the facts head-on is an informed way to cope through a problem.

Consider also the way denial can be beneficial. Never thought about it that way? What about refusing to accept failure as the final answer? You can rebuff the idea of being denied what you believe you deserve. You can deny accepting something that stands in the way of your happiness. Think of stories you've heard about people surviving extraordinary circumstances because they denied the possibility of any other outcome. There are countless accounts of miraculous recoveries from near-fatal accidents and catastrophic events. A common strategy in overcoming tragedy is deciding not to accept the worst. Parents of children with mental and or physical disabilities often use denial in the form of a steadfast refusal to give up or accept less for their child. The positive use of denial can span the scope of the catastrophic to the subtle.

I worked with a family struggling with their responsibilities for their elderly mother, Martha. The children, Dan and Susan, were having a difficult time getting Martha to agree to some gradual changes. They carefully navigated the new and necessary territory of adjusting her driving habits, getting help with the household chores and implementing safe internet practices. Some were easier than others. Susan became particularly distraught when Martha announced she intended to get a new puppy. Susan voiced her frustration to Dan that getting a pet with a life expectancy longer than its owner was unfair to the dog and to the ones left to care for it. Susan was incredulous that their mother couldn't see the impracticality. It seemed particularly dubious to Susan that Martha, who was a complainer about anything that required much of her attention, would want such an obligation and complication in her life.

Susan wanted Dan to acknowledge that Martha was in denial. He did, but he was insightful enough to recognize Martha's obstinance had nothing to do with wanting a dog and everything to do with her resolve to deny that she was nearing the time she would lose her autonomy. In her mind, getting a dog meant she had time left. She would be the caregiver instead of the one in need of care. Her denial represented her resistance to losing her independence.

Susan and Dan were both correct about the reality; they were reasonably concerned. Yet Martha had every right to feel as she did as well. The compromise was to take Martha to the local shelter for some "scouting trips" to look at possible adoptees. As Dan predicted, Martha wasn't really ready to commit, so this exercise gave her a way to say it was a possibility without obligation. The folks who ran the shelter enjoyed her visits so much that they asked her to become a regular volunteer. This workable solution benefited everyone. Martha got out of the house and interacted with people. It gave her a feeling of being useful. She relished her new status as tour guide and helping match adoptees with their new families. Her denial was not harmful in any way and was a coping skill that helped her transition to a new phase of life on her terms.

Denial can come to you in the form of rejection. You didn't get something or someone in your life. You couldn't remove a barrier in your pursuit of your goals. The denial can lead to disappointment and can move into depression.

What if the denial is in place for a reason. What if that reason you were denied was a way of the universe telling you *not this* because there is *something better*?

Rejection is *redirection*.

Think for a moment of the times *no* turned out to be the right answer. Think of ways *no* meant *not now* because *later was better*. Let the no be the path to yes.

Rejection is *protection*.

Now think of ways you were disappointed because something didn't work out, you didn't get something you wanted, you missed what you thought was an opportunity. Then you realized later after the event that you might have been harmed in some way. You were late getting to appointment but the delay prevented you from being in the wreck that happened in the very spot you travel. You missed the plane that went down on takeoff. Or maybe it's less dramatic and the guy who dumped you turned out to be a serial cheater or the company that didn't hire you went out of business two years later.

Assigning an emotion to a word can limit its power or give it more than it deserves. You get to decide.

There are certain words that are keys for you. They open doors of possibility. They are ways for you to take charge.

Say *I will* instead of *I'll try*.

Will affirms success.

Try acknowledges and entertains a possibility of failure.

Some words are magnets that attract the positive.

Say *when this happens* instead of *if this happens*.

When promises action.

If stifles opportunity.

This may sound like a lesson in semantics, but I urge you to consider it seriously. Think of how someone has said something to you in a way that hit your brain like a thunderbolt. It may have been something you already knew, but the messenger brought it to you in a new way. Or maybe you'd heard it before, but the words grabbed your attention and your heartstrings. The words they chose were exactly what you needed to hear to connect your head to your heart.

No matter what anybody tells you, words and ideas can change the world.

—John Keating

You can do this for yourself. You can alter your life by altering your narrative. Breathe life into it with the words you speak. Flesh it out into a whole and real entity that can be used to move you forward. Build with your words. Construct and create. Change your thoughts to change your life. You've heard that before. It's absolutely true. Your thoughts need action to give them life. It takes intent, diligence, patience, vigilance, and self-mercy. When you set your intent to change your thoughts to change your direction, begin by changing your words. It is a simple alteration that only takes a few moments of your time the instant you speak.

The beauty of this strategy is you don't have to believe it yet. Speak it as if it is so. After doing that a while, start to imagine how it would feel if those words were your reality. Associating that emotional feeling with those words makes them like rocket boosters. They will catapult you forward. We'll talk about ways for you to use words effectively when we discuss optimum coping skills, but as you talk about the problem currently in your life, notice the words you use. You may not be ready to do more. Remembering that words do matter is an important step.

This is the first place you can begin to find your workable solution.

You've invested in this book and I've promised you concrete strategies, so let's talk about what you're facing. You'll notice that I avoid using loaded words like right and wrong or better and worse. My goal is to urge you to assign your own qualifiers for what you desire. Your wants are what matter here. Dig deep to mine for the words. Search for the ones that best tell your story.

I have only one steadfast, non-negotiable rule for problem-solving. There is one word I ask you to be intentionally mindful about.

Always Say *The* Problem, Not *My* Problem.

If you claim a problem as yours, you bestow it with abilities. You allow it to direct you, dictate your feelings and actions. You submit to it. You surrender before you even begin to fight. Take some of the sting from a problem by separating from it in this simple way.

Don't claim it. Don't let it claim you. It will grab hold, seep down within you, take root, and grow like kudzu. If you know about kudzu, you're familiar with the thick, climbing, clinging vine that invasively covers and then smothers everything in its path. Whatever it grows on becomes buried underneath. If you aren't familiar with kudzu then search it online. You'll see photos of huge green leaves on coiled and twisted vines. Once these vines have a hold they don't let go.

In the same way, if you allow it, a problem will overtake you so completely that after a while, you'll no longer recognize who you are without it. Those around you will begin to see you as the one with that problem as well.

Don't allow it to become part of your identity.

If the problem becomes ingrained in you, then efforts to change that perception will be all the more difficult. It will be hard to see yourself differently and hard for the other people in your life. That adds another problem to the problem.

You must resist the temptation to declare ownership of any problem. So often people will say, *my* weight problem, *my* cancer, *my* addiction, *my* depression, *my* OCD.

Instead, neutralize it with the word *the*. This is another great coping skill to help manage the stress of the problem.

I want you to tell me about the problem you're facing right now. It may be a bump in your road, or it may be that you've careened off a cliff. Imagine we're having a private conversation in your favorite restaurant, bar, or coffee shop. Say what you need to say to outline the situation. Express your feelings with glorious powerful words. Tell me the situation, the players, and the emotions. We'll look for what part you've played, not as blame but for how recognizing it can help you focus on possible opportunities that can move the obstacles standing in your way.

It's strategy time.

5 STEPS
FOR COPING SMART

CHAPTER SIX:

YOU'VE ALREADY STARTED

Let's talk about how all of this we've discussed is going to help you with the current problem in your life in a concrete, measurable way. We've used the analogy of a roadmap as instructions to get you to your definition of happiness and success. The insights you've gained in the previous chapters are the guideposts available to you. They tell you where you've been and how far you've come. That information is essential to know how far you still have to go to get to your desired destination.

Let's use another analogy.

A blueprint.

Think about a blueprint. It resembles an X-ray. It's a look inside the walls of a structure. You can see what can't be seen with the naked eye. The hundreds of supporting lines and angles and arches are like a skeleton. That's why we refer to the "bones" of a house.

Architecture relies on mathematical principles. The numbers have to add up or the structure will collapse. A blueprint provides intricately detailed instructions. It illustrates the most granular details—many of which are internal but vital to the finished product and its functionality. Everything you need to know to successfully construct the end result is there. Every consideration for workability is met and satisfied and revealed.

I love the idea of building anything. It's proactive and productive.

It can be creative and imaginative. It results in a tangible visual. Isn't that your goal?

To make your vision a reality.

To see your dreams come true.

To build the life you want without the problem and the stress it's causing.

Sounds good, right? It may also sound a lot like all the positivity thrown at you lately. Pundits, celebrities, your mom, your Facebook friends, Pinterest, and on and on it comes. It all sounds good but doesn't feel good long enough. So now you're ready to see something concrete happen. You've begun Coping Smart already. Let's see what that looks like so far.

In Chapter One, we talked about your family legacy. As a blueprint reveals the essential framing within the walls of a structure, think of that family legacy as the frame for the design of you. Your family is the support beams for your inner walls.

You examined your wiring for personality and temperament in Chapter Two. A blueprint details the intricate wiring system needed to provide a power source for a structure. That's what your personality does for you.

A blueprint is the stamp of architectural design style of a structure. Shape, line, pattern, texture, and space are all elements. The way they are used and interpreted is the key to the design value we assign them. There are Modern, Postmodern, Mediterranean, Italianate, Arts & Craft, Deco, Classical, Baroque, Federalist, Gothic, Tudor, and many more styles to choose from when building a structure. In Chapter Three, you examined the experiences that have come with your location on your life road and determined how they have shaped you. Chapter Four was an honest review of your relationships and how they provide key elements of your emotional style. That's the design of you.

You've done a lot of the work to see what lies within. Looking at your legacy, your wiring, your experiences, and the quality of your relationships is like a building inspection. It's a chance to examine and discover any stress fractures and weak spots in the early construction that need reinforcement so that what you build next stands strong. Then you get to pick all the fun design elements; the colors and embellishments that put your stamp on the finished product.

I want to help you design and build the life you want.

Anyone who has ever built a house knows the headaches involved. It doesn't happen by itself or by chance. There's a master plan that requires hard work, creativity, patience, resilience to setbacks, and a determination for it to become a reality. You can't do it alone. You rely on others to do their part. Some perform as agreed and some don't. You're left to deal with the fallout when people fail you. Some begin at your side and then abandon you. They make promises that they break. They may remain with you but don't do their part and invest the same time and effort as you in the relationship. There are predictable problems that arise and some that you don't see coming.

The core belief of Coping Smart is not all problems are solvable but they are manageable.

Read that again.

Not all problems are solvable, but they are manageable.

There is a workable solution available to you to overcome the problem and get out from under the stress. It may not solve the problem completely. I know that and you do, too. You can't "fix" a broken heart. When someone dies, no one can bring them back. There are physical conditions that can't be repaired. The list goes on. But there are always options to make any situation workable in some way. You can heal from heartache and love again. You can honor a loved one who has died by living your life with joy. You can find ways to move past physical limitations with your other abilities and your spirit. If you have a void of any kind in your life you can fill that place with service. A sure way to receive what you need is to offer it to others. You get what you give.

So, where do you start? The good news is you've already started. It began the moment you opened this book, your mind and your heart.

To find a workable solution, you must first identify the nature of the problem.

How do you do that? Why would you want to do that? A problem is a problem, right?

No.

Problems come in all sizes.

I will help you identify and rate the severity and impact of the problem you're facing. Why do you need to do this? Not all problems are the same. I mentioned this earlier in the Introduction. Problems are as unique to you as your fingerprints. All of those factors we've discussed including your legacy, wiring, experiences and relationships influence how you view a problem. Just as people are different, their responses to problems differ. It doesn't matter how anyone else might handle this problem, the only thing that matters is how *you* manage this problem.

It may feel out of your control, but how much of your emotional energy you devote to a particular difficulty is in your hands. It's another choice you have that you might not have realized is yours to make. You're bogged down in the muck of a difficulty. Think of it as traction to get you unstuck and moving forward. Even if someone else is part of the story, you get to write the scenes and decide how big their role will be from here on. Take that and use it.

We have learned as a society to supersize everything. Bigger is better. Reality television has emphasized our fascination with drama. We've come to expect and value overreaction. Is that what you want for your own life? Do you want the problem to be bigger, the discomfort to be more uncomfortable, the fallout to be more devastating, and the impact to be longer-lasting than necessary?

To manage the problem, you also need to identify and clarify your options. This is take-back-your-power time. This is where options are dependent upon examining possible consequences. Rather than allowing things to happen to you, it is possible to direct the outcome by your choices.

Next, the real relief begins. You can devise a plan that checks the boxes for you, satisfies your needs, and leads you to your idea of peace with regard to your situation.

You know by now from reading this book that I am a champion of celebration. I believe with all my soul that any size celebration is a profound coping mechanism. Life sucks in so many ways that you have to remind yourself it is also glorious in just as many. Look for every single possible reason to applaud your efforts. Cumulatively, they will carry you where you want to go. You're reading this book. You're opening yourself to the questions that are the clues on the treasure map. They will show you the way.

There is no limit on the fabulousness of life. No rule that says only this person or that one can participate or advance to the top of the mountain. The mountain doesn't choose who climbs it. Turn off the naysaying in your head wherever it originates. You're about to take this problem in your life, put it in perspective, and find a way to leave it in your dust.

So there's a lot ahead we're going to talk about. I promised you specific steps. I'm going to walk through them with you. I'm going to make this as clear and as rewarding as possible for all your efforts.

Let's recap what you've already accomplished!

You have:

- Made a decision to seek help to cope with the problem in your life.

- Identified the "whys" of who you are to become wise with insight and empathy.

- Identified your personality traits that work for you and the ones that aren't serving you.

- Recognized that behavior doesn't simply happen. It's your choice.

- Taken time to acknowledge your opportunity to take charge for change.

- Considered success as making the effort not only the end result.

- Recognized that staying positive is hard work.

- Decided to find concrete ways to make the abstract concept of positivity real and effective.

- Identified your deal-breakers by determining what is acceptable and unacceptable in your life.

- Mapped your location on your life roadmap.

- Recognized the importance of choosing your words with care.

- Drawn the relationships circle of your life and clarified the positions of importance of the people in it.

- Examined the perspective viewpoint of others who influence and potentially affect your quality of life.

- Distinguished the difference between being judgmental and making a judgement call.

- Learned how denial can be detrimental avoidance or it can be a refusal to fail.

- Clarified the difference between your passion and your purpose.

- Opened up to the possibility that problems present possibilities.

Look at all you've done so far. You've started sketching the blueprint you'll need by thoughtfully examining all of the issues, you've formed the foundation for the life you want. You've looked at the structural integrity.

You're on the road and on your way.

Now we're going to talk about the specific steps you can take to reclaim and sustain your emotional equilibrium. You're going to discover how to identify the problem and the feelings, clarify your options, manage the stress, find your workable solution.

You're about to change your life and set the direction YOU choose.

CHAPTER SEVEN:

STEP 1. STOP & THINK

Something happened to alter your landscape. Maybe it was devasting. Maybe, it wasn't quite so overwhelming. You didn't get the promotion, you just bought a new house and your partner has been transferred to another state, your upstairs neighbor keeps playing music until two in the morning, or your air conditioner needs replacing on a sweltering day in August but you don't have the five thousand dollars it costs to replace it.

You might be experiencing an overall sense of dissatisfaction. You can't quite name it.

Ask yourself this question. How bad is this problem you're facing?

The first step is to stop for a moment and think about the severity of the problem. Why? Because this is where you get to decide what will work for you to relieve the discomfort of the situation and how much emotional energy you're going to invest in this difficulty. This is so vital that you see the theme here. You feel out of control. This problem feels bigger than you. Someone else is causing the difficulty. All those ways you described the problem, are important. Listen to the adjectives you used. They tell the story and assign emotions to the facts. I want you to understand from the get-go, that you aren't power*less* or help*less*.

You aren't *less* in any way.

Problems range in severity, length, consequences, and possible outcomes. Some have very obvious solutions. Like an elegant equation, if you have A then B happens you can then do C to achieve your desired outcome of D. Even if the solution is difficult to attain, the answer is at least clear. You know what is required of you to solve the problem. You decide whether you are willing to do it.

It isn't always so easy. Not all problems have such a straightforward solution. Some may not have an evident or a satisfactory answer. I know that may be important to you now, but you'll soon see what really matters is getting out from under the stress.

Relief.

Let's find some for you. By deciding how much you need, you'll determine what to do. Is this problem as big as you think it is?

I want you to read out loud what you wrote down when I asked you to tell me about this problem. Pay attention again to the words you used. Think about them a moment. Do you hear those factors of your legacy, wiring, experiences, and relationships speaking their parts? They will remain part of this process but because you recognize they're there, you can now determine how much they will influence you from here forward.

I use four categories that help rate the severity of any problem. Some problems are mildly irritating and only a blip on your radar. Some are pervasive and affect everything you do. Once you evaluate the severity of the problem, you can practice what I call emotional conservation. This is the equivalent of going green in your emotional life. Conserve your emotional reserves. The amount of energy and effort you expend, your strength to withstand stress, and your resilience to difficulty are those reserves. You need to save them for the times you will need them most. Then, the less stressful things won't deplete you.

In your emotional life, think about sustainability. Can you resist the lure of drama of a big reaction? Do you want to? Should you sustain drama for the long haul or save yourself the stress? To do this, stop and think before you make a judgment. Then you can choose a response wisely. Can you sustain calm by thinking about the size of the problem and deciding to react and respond accordingly? This is Step One.

By stopping for a moment to examine a problem, you can decide which of four categories applies. Then you can choose a reaction that is equitable to the situation and worthy of your emotional investment.

Here are the four specific categories of a problem and the criteria for each. All problems fall into these categories.

- **Complication.** This is a problem that is an inconvenience or a possible source of aggravation. These happen every day and often multiple times a day. Attitude and perspective are key.

- **Dilemma.** This is a problem that is larger in scope and usually has at least two clear options. These are either-or situations that require action based on reasoning for those choices.

- **Crisis.** This is a problem that is much more serious in its potential for major impact. It requires more than an attitude adjustment. Analytical thinking is necessary to make a critical decision. This calls for management strategy.

- **Tragedy.** This is a situation that, once set into motion by you or someone else or forces beyond your control, cannot be changed by any amount of action or reaction on your part. It is unquestionably life-altering. It requires monumental effort from you to affect the scope of the impact and eventual outcome for your emotional wellness.

I know you're saying, okay, that makes some sense. Certainly, some problems are a bigger deal than others. But how does that process of determining severity work, and why does it work? Why should you adopt this process in all problem solving?

Let's break it down.

I'll give an example of each category with a scenario. This example problem happens to Sam. (I use that name and the pronoun *they* so you can identify Sam with any gender you wish.) In these scenarios, I'm going to use the same basic situation and let the problem escalate to illustrate distinct differences for each category and how Sam's chosen reaction affects the outcome.

A COMPLICATION

Sam's driving to the airport to pick up their company's most important client for the annual stockholders' meeting. It's raining. Sam's car has a flat tire on the highway. They realize that they must get out and change the tire on the busy highway in the pouring rain. They get the tire changed and arrive at the airport soaking wet, agitated, and flustered. This has them so off their game that Sam blows a golden opportunity to charm and impress the VIP client one-on-one during the half-hour long ride to the corporate office. The conversation is wasted on the weather instead.

A DILEMMA

Sam's driving to the airport to pick up an important client for the company presentation. Sam's car has a flat tire. They pull over, get out in the rain, walk back to the rear of the car, and open the trunk. There's no spare. They realize their partner forgot to replace it from the last repair. This complication has now escalated to the next level. Sam must make an either-or decision. They can call for roadside assistance in the hopes that help will come quickly in the rain and heavy traffic or call the office and make other arrangements for someone else to pick up the client on time. Sam worries about fallout from their boss if they fail to be the one to be there to get the client, so Sam makes the choice to call for roadside assistance. As they wait, Sam calls their partner to berate them for their carelessness. Angry and an hour late, Sam arrives at the airport, too irritated to put their feelings aside and effectively engage with the client who is now totally disgruntled.

A CRISIS

Sam's driving to the airport to pick up a VIP client for an important meeting and has to deal with a flat tire on a busy highway in the rain. Sam realizes their partner used the spare and didn't replace it. Now Sam's really angry and frustrated. They must decide whether to call roadside assistance for help or the office to dispatch a colleague to get the client. Sam panics at the thought of the wrath of their demanding boss, so they call roadside service and don't alert the office of the delay. The weather and traffic detain the repair truck for what seems like eternity. An anxiety-wrought Sam arrives at the airport to find the angry client called to the office to complain about Sam's no-show and has been picked up by a car service after waiting over an hour. When Sam gets back to the office, they remain anxious and angry. They become defensive when confronted by their irate boss. They make excuses blaming their partner and become belligerent. The boss berates Sam for incompetence and fires them on the spot. On the way home Sam realizes they have not only lost their job, but their health insurance benefits that cover their child's cystic fibrosis treatments.

A TRAGEDY

Sam's driving to the airport to retrieve an important client, their car has a flat tire on a busy highway in the rain, and there's no spare in the trunk. Sam becomes angry and paces back and forth. Then Sam begins to panic at the idea of getting in trouble with their boss and strides back toward the front of the car to retrieve their phone to call for help. Distracted by their rage, Sam doesn't realize they're too close to the traffic and is hit by an oncoming vehicle. Sam wakes up in the hospital days later to find they have been paralyzed in the accident, altering their life and lifestyle forever.

I know this seems drastic to take a problem from the inconvenient to the unthinkable, but stay with me. Now look at each scenario. You can see the escalating severity. It may be shocking to think of these potential problems together, as they are so different in scope of damage. That's the point. In each, there was a moment to stop the action and think before choosing a reaction that would have altered the outcome.

Even when the problem is mundane or seems innocuous, your response has an effect. You can save yourself from being angry and from the possibility for the problem to escalate simply by taking a minute to stop and think about what's happening, how you feel about it, and most importantly, what you're about to do next.

Like most everyone, you've grown accustomed to thinking in that super-sized perception we talked about, including your reaction to the things in your life that go awry. The hectic pace of life exposes you to all sorts of aggravation. Everything feels like a big deal. You feel raw and the feeling dictates so much of the drama around you.

We have all developed a hyper-sensitivity to drama. Interestingly, rather than being turned off by it we are drawn to it. That's why reality television is so seductive, why influencers and critics become disproportionately relevant, and why Facebook and Instagram and all social media platforms pervade and persuade.

Drama is fed by emotion. Emotions thrive on thrills and chaos.

You have the ability to take it down a notch, lessen the fallout, and possibly avoid the problem altogether.

Let's look at the scenarios for each type of problem. We'll examine Sam's actions. Then we'll talk about the experiences and emotions as they occurred in each category.

The Complication

Here there was an opportunity for choice. Sam was dealt a situation not of their making, but they had complete control of how they reacted. A complication is mountain or mole hill time. Sam allowed it to knock them off kilter for dealing with the VIP client and made a bad impression. What could Sam do differently for a different outcome?

They could stop and think before they do anything.

This would give Sam a moment to collect themselves, make a decision, and adjust their attitude to meet the assignment and seize the chance to prevail. The stop action would keep Sam in control of what happens next and more importantly give them the opportunity to think about how they choose to feel about it, which in turn would affect the rest of their experience and its outcome. See the domino effect? It can go further and have more implications. We don't know what Sam did after the company event. Maybe they allowed their frustration and anger to remain and took it home to their partner and maybe their kids affecting everyone's quality of life from that one original problem moment.

What could Sam do that would produce a different outcome? A more productive approach would have been for Sam to recover their composure, ditch the feeling of aggravation, use their personality and charm to woo the VIP client and thereby win favor with the boss. See how the escalation can go either way and the choices were Sam's to make? What if that client had been so impressed by Sam that it led to Sam being offered a new position with the client's firm?

How many times have you had a similar situation? You know you reacted in a way that made things worse. These are knee-jerk reflexes when you act before your reasoning mind catches up. You kick up the drama. Think of the times that you have also been affected by someone else's situation when they made it into a larger issue. It was easy to see how they should have reacted. When you stop and think, it's easier to see how you can respond more favorably.

Life is full of surprises, frustrations, and annoyances. They can color your world or rock it. Problems can gain momentum in the blink of an eye if you give them more weight than they merit.

Let's apply the category of complication to your life. Your dog develops a bladder infection and has to be walked at 3:00 a.m. every day for six weeks. You realize an hour before your best friend's wedding that your rental tux is the wrong size. You're invited to a dinner party unaware that it's the hostess's birthday party and you arrive with no gift. Maybe you can recall a complication that you have dealt with lately. Can you see how the result was determined by your response? Stop and think about the perspective of severity when you compare these problems to a larger one in scope.

- How is this going to impact this moment?

- How much impact can you determine with an attitude shift?

- What matters most, the momentary emotion or the outcome?

- Is a different result worth a different response?

Challenge yourself to look at how that change can put you back in control.

The Dilemma

Choices here are very specific and action-oriented. Sam lost sight of the task at hand and let anger rule reason. They wasted time and energy fuming instead of strategizing. Their need to satisfy their anger caused them to be distracted from a constructive plan, and strike out at and injure their partner in a blindside verbal attack. Blame became the choice instead of resourcefulness. That obscured the task at hand and began the descent into trouble. What could Sam have done instead? They had a choice to stop and think about the price of choosing anger over calm and focus. They could dial it down with a clear-headed decision. Sam could have shifted the dynamic completely. It was in their hands.

A dilemma requires reasoning. You're confronted with a door number one or door number two type of choice. It may be like in this scenario where a momentary decision must be made, or it may go on for a longer time. Should you risk driving through that caution light because you're running late and gamble you won't get caught by a policeman or, worse, have a wreck? Do you leave your sleeping child in the bed while you walk the dog? Maybe your dilemma is whether to take a job in another city and move your family from the home they've known. It could be trying to decide if you should cut back your work hours and go back to school. You may be exploring staying in a comfortable relationship that isn't fulfilling your needs or to pursue the unknown. Consider these questions:

- What are your either-or choices in this situation?

- What are the possible results of both?

115

- Are the possible results of little consequence or are they serious in impact?

- Will the results play out in someone else's story in a way you're willing to gamble on?

- If the possible outcome is of a serious nature, could it set off a domino tumble of all you have worked hard to build?

- Will it inhibit you from moving forward or set you free to design the life you really want?

The Crisis

In this scenario, Sam let emotion dictate their behavior and blind them to more constructive options. Anxiety overrode their better judgment and escalated the problem. What could they have done instead? They could have taken a moment to stop and think of the impact of giving their emotions free reign. They could have been the one to call the car service to assure the client was taken care of smoothly, guaranteeing their arrival at the meeting on time. That may have elevated Sam in the eyes of their boss as quick-thinking, resourceful, and dependable. It would have solved the immediate problem of getting the client to the meeting on time and lessened the impact of the flat tire problem.

The solution could have gone further. There was also a way for Sam to mitigate the damage even after the fiasco. Instead of confronting the boss while still angry, they could have accepted responsibility and made an earnest effort to save their position. Even if losing their job remained as the outcome, Sam would know that they had taken control of their emotions and made the available effort. Chosen behavior was an option throughout the situation. Sam had opportunities to direct the impact from beginning to end.

It's important to note that the chance to take back the narrative goes even further. Once Sam followed through in a way that resulted in the termination from that job, they must decide what to do next. We'll talk about next steps in more detail later, but for the purpose of learning to discover your ability to gain clarity, note that even after a huge setback, a decision can still be made to move forward. Sam could ask for a meeting with the boss to take ownership and apologize for their mistake. This may not lead to reinstatement, though there's that chance, and may not help at all, but it could result in receiving a more favorable climate for their exit and networking possibilities for a future with another company. Also, the temptation to let this blow knock them to their knees can be managed with proactive thinking for a remedy. The crisis is escalated by a new problem with the loss of insurance coverage. There is no time for staying stuck in the aftermath. The new problem calls for another decision. Sam can allow themselves to be set back with failure or to use it as a stepping-stone to the future and pursue a new job quickly.

A crisis must be met with focused strategies to minimize the effect. This category of problem requires more than recognition and attitude. This is sink or swim, look before you leap, use your head time. It may call for a Hail Mary pass maneuver.

There is usually an additional problem in a crisis. It affects the people around you. This calls for consideration beyond your needs or wishes. You've begun to abuse that pain medication and it's putting your family's well-being in jeopardy. You bought a new house then quit your job. Your doctor tells you either stop drinking or die of cirrhosis.

The crisis in your life may not be of your making. Often this means you must manage something that you didn't initiate. Your partner abandoned you with a newborn, and you have no income. Your company relocates and you must move or lose your job. Your child is using drugs and failing school. It could be that life deals you a blow that was separate from anything you or anyone did. You've been diagnosed with cancer.

A crisis is breeding ground for panic and anxiety. They'll rush you and threaten your ability to cope. They'll hamper or halt clarity and insight. Awareness of that threat is imperative to your strategic survival. Preparation is your best defense. It makes these factors less scary. Know that panic and anxiety are persistent and pervasive and very common reactions to stress. When you acknowledge the threat, it can minimize the effect. Here's the operative word again that I want you to hold on to with every fiber of your being.

Manageable.

You might not always get to the why, but the *what can I do next* is always there. This is the action part that gets you moving even if it's one tiny shuffle of a step at a time. Isn't that what you really want? To get somewhere other than here where it hurts? Don't you want to be focused on something other than this difficulty?

The Tragedy

The last category I use to identify the nature of a problem is the easiest to spot. You know heartache and grief when you see it. There's also a universal common response. The problem scenario with Sam strikes a chord. Most everyone has a deep-seated fear of this sort of occurrence happening in their life to them or someone they love. It's a very realistic fear that life can be altered in a split second. It is also an inevitable fact that these events do happen, and the reason why is likely never revealed. You may have played some part in the event or it may have been totally beyond your control. Tragedy often seems random. That's really scary.

Tragedies bring grief. They are inseparable partners. The resulting grief and profound sadness from a death isn't reserved only for the end of a human life. It can be the death of a love relationship, a friendship, an expectation, a dream. These are also tragic in impact.

Now look what you wrote down when you told me about your problem. Consider the four categories.

- Which category describes the problem you're facing?

- Does thinking of it in this analytical way give you some distance so you can begin to think critically toward a solution?

- Does rating the problem give you a feeling of having some control over it?

- Do you see something you can do or could have done differently to make a difference?

Breaking a problem down into a category helps you clarify your perspective. Perspective is the value you assign a situation using all of the factors that shape who you are that we've discussed.

Perspective is formed in multiple and often subtle ways. Yours can broadly affect your view of problems. I use Miriam's story to illustrate how perspective can literally cause a specific problem situation. At age fifty, Miriam had never learned to swim. The thought of putting her face underneath the water terrified her. It was a fact that embarrassed her, so she didn't tell anyone except her husband Calvin. It became an issue over the years when Calvin's firm gave cruise trips as rewards for sales performance and mandated corporate events. Miriam didn't want to him to miss out so she rationalized that being *on* the water was safe. Being *in* the water was dangerous she thought. She got so good at telling herself it was okay that she even supported Calvin's decision to buy a family ski boat and she accompanied him on weekend outings.

One summer evening at a neighbor's backyard cookout and pool party, Miriam decided to join in the pool fun at the urging of several people who noticed she was on the sidelines. She took advantage of a large raft floating in the shallow end near the crowd. She used her standby rationalization that because she was on the water, she was safe. She was floating along enjoying the conversation when a neighbor swimming nearby decided he couldn't resist an opportunity to pull a prank. Unaware she couldn't swim, the neighbor went underneath the raft and dumped Miriam off and into the water. In an instant she was face down in the water and thrashing wildly as the others roared with laughter. Suddenly, she stopped flailing and sank to the bottom. Calvin jumped in and rescued her. Everyone was stunned into silence. Miriam began to cough up water and gave the crowd a thumbs up that she was okay. They were relieved but a bit confused. Later Calvin asked Miriam what had happened. She was drowning she replied. Didn't she realize he asked, that all she had to do was stand up?

Miriam had allowed the problem to be magnified before she thought it through. In her mind the simple tumble into the water became a matter of life and death. She let her fear of embarrassment that the crowd would find her out and her fear of the water skew her perspective of the problem. Those emotions took over her better sense. The water was only three feet deep. If she had stopped panicking and thought about it, she would have realized she was in the shallow end and out of danger.

I use her story to illustrate the importance of taking a moment to stop and get the problem into perspective. Think it through. It may be a true crisis or a tragedy, and you'll need to respond accordingly as we'll discuss. In evaluating the severity of a complication or a dilemma it bears asking yourself a question. Is it as severe as it might seem at first glance?

Don't allow yourself to drown in the shallow end.

CHAPTER EIGHT:

STEP 2. GET ON TOP OF THE EMOTIONS

Emotions measure your conscious connection to your place in the world. They telegraph messages from your head to your heart. Along the way they activate and involve your entire nervous system. It may feel like it starts in your heart or perhaps your gut, but your emotions lie waiting in your brain. In a flash they can zing you. That can be a wanted and welcomed surge or a disarming one.

Step Two is all about identifying the emotions in any problem situation. The range of possible emotions you are feeling in response to the difficulty you're having is wide and deep. You're hurt. You're angry. You're lost. You're confused. You're worn out. You're crushed. You're humiliated. You're jealous. You're resentful. You're disappointed. You're heartsick. You're disgusted. You're discouraged. You're scared.

Then there are all the negative admonishments you receive that are associated with emotions and assign judgment to what you're feeling.

You're too emotional.

Your emotions get in the way.

Don't let your emotions get the best of you.

You're blinded by emotion.

Don't get carried away by your emotions.

You're an emotional wreck.

It's as if your emotions are all undesirable. Right now, the ones that are taunting you are ones that are causing you discomfort.

Emotions are also the parts of you that are magical, mystical, and marvelous. You know the feeling of joy, elation, love, contentment, satisfaction, attraction, appreciation, hope, devotion and bliss. You spend your life seeking them. Those positive feelings are the rewards for all your efforts to make the most of your life.

Emotions are the catalysts for behavior. You're motivated to do because of what you feel. You're also motivated by what you believe emotions are capable of making you feel. That means they are a power source to be managed. They can send you toward your desired goals and keep you moving forward. Conversely, they can seduce you into detours along the road that leads to dead ends or worse, a sink hole, or worst of all over a cliff.

The key is to learn how to discern which emotions are constructive and which are destructive. Then they become coping skills in problem-solving.

The danger with emotions is their ability to be shape-shifters. Fear morphs into anger. Love can transform into obsession. Anticipation can become anxiety. Admiration shifts to jealousy. Positivity can mask pain. Expectancy can lead to resentment.

Let your emotions serve you, not sway you.

How many times have you told yourself or others that you can't help the way you feel? Emotions, especially the potentially negative ones, come on you and course through you in a blink. Your brain receives the undesirable information and converts it to messages that hit your gut with a visceral pang, bottom out deep down, then surge back up to your brain where they ping against your skull in a ritual kind of familiar warning. I liken it to a pinball machine. Something happens or someone does something that elicits a negative response from you. Their behavior is the action that pulls the plunger back and shoots the ball of emotion throughout your body. Alarms go off. Warning lights flash. You start batting away at the feelings until you get them to stop.

Some people think of emotions in terms of a set laws whose properties and principles are accepted as predictable and fixed. You assume you'll feel a certain way about someone or something. That has a great deal to do with those factors of you that provide the prescription of the lens you view the world through. Your emotions have a history. That's why emotions are really more like art than science. They are as subjective and as varied as the human experience and imagination.

Emotions, like energy, are kinetic. They move and shift and accelerate and fade and pulse and rage and recede. When a tsunami of emotion washes over you and knocks you to the floor, it's hard to imagine standing against it. Think of the weather reporters you've seen doing their job literally holding on for their physical safety against the elements in a natural disaster. Stand your ground. You must form a mental barrier to dam off the flood of emotions.

Sometimes an emotion is a nagging presence you wish would go away. Try thinking of it as a habit you want to change. You have to be vigilant and watch for triggers to break the pattern.

Your emotional energy is both mental and physical. You know how exhausting dealing with difficulty is and the toll it takes on your body and your mind. You can't separate the two. Your mind is the motherboard of your computer body. The emotional coding you use as input determines how your body performs. Emotions can boost your power or act as a virus that spreads and infects your information.

Let's take it back to our road of life analogy. Emotions can be rocks on the road. You may have been going too fast or swerved too close to the shoulder and one flew up and hit your windshield. Someone else may have passed you and flung the rock. Either way it causes damage. It can be a small ping that's a minor issue or a crack that goes across your entire line of vision and distorts your view.

More powerful emotions are also like potholes. When you hit one you feel the jolt all over. It doesn't stop you from continuing from moving forward, but it does cause you to pause to gather yourself mentally. On some stretches of road, you remain tense and worried in anticipation of another. This is that anxiety you feel. It can quickly take the enjoyment out of the journey.

The really big emotions have the potential to run you off the road completely. It can be a blow-out, and you find yourself on the side of the road. Or an obstacle of another vehicle, person, is in your path that causes you to swerve. These are the boulders that crush you in a landslide. Then there are the ones that end in a ditch. The most devastating result can be a tumble down the ravine. You get the idea.

Here's the kicker. Emotion travels faster in your brain than reason. Let me say that again.

The speed of emotion is faster than the speed of reason.

The feeling will always hit your brain before you have a chance to think it through. This is why Step One is so critical. Think of it as a time-out. The time-out strategy works for kids because the physical distance removes them mentally from the situation. It allows their minds to catch up and process the feeling and the facts. Without realizing it parents are using the Stop and Think step if they utilize a time-out and are laying the foundation of a healthy coping skill for life.

(Quick parenting tip here: I would suggest time-out be presented to a child as a coping skill rather than a punishment. Being sent to your room for unacceptable behavior should be a clear consequence. A time-out's purpose should be for aiding a child in impulse control and reasoning.)

As an adult you can remove yourself from the emotion of a difficult moment by taking a breath and mentally pausing. There are times when actually leaving the room can be helpful for you, too. I've spent many hours in my car driving around the neighborhood alternating from screaming to crying where no one else could hear. You may have your own method to distance yourself while you think things through. As long as what you choose doesn't harm you or anyone else it's okay. I worked with a client who had a unique approach. She purchased several boxes of glassware at a garage sale and stored them away for such situations. Whenever she needed to get her emotions in line she would go outside, grab a box, walk out into the backyard, and throw glasses one by one against her garage wall. No one got hurt, and she felt better.

Find your method.

Ask yourself these questions instead of accepting emotions as they come.

- Can you name the emotion you are currently feeling?

- Is it serving you or swaying you?

- Was it predictable?

- If it was unexpected can you identify the source?

- How much energy have you spent on the emotion of this situation?

- How much more emotional energy are you willing to invest?

- Has that investment cost you physically as well?

- Is that emotional and physical cost interfering with your quality of life?

- Is it diminishing your ability to function in your daily routine?

- Does that deficit apply to your relationships as well?

- Do you see a way you might reframe the situation to change it?

- Do you want to sustain the emotions you're feeling?

- What emotions would you prefer to renew?

- Are you willing to go green and conserve emotional energy?

- Can you think of ways to distance from an undesirable emotion and neutralize it?

There is also a threat to your emotional well-being if you allow the emotion to become a default setting. It can easily become your comfort zone. You can be in the throes of that emotion so long that it becomes part of your identity to yourself and others. Dictate your emotions rather than allowing them to direct you. You don't have to be that angry guy or that drama queen. That's your choice as well.

You will always have feelings.

Distancing from them in order to manage them effectively doesn't mean you stop having feelings. You can, however, intentionally and deliberately choose more constructive feelings as well as constructive ways to show them. Decide to replace the feelings of distress with more productive emotions.

Let me take a moment here to assure you that I'm not discounting what you are feeling.

You feel what you feel. Period.

I honor and validate where you are and the emotions that are surrounding you. Emotions come for all the reasons we've discussed.

I'm not telling you what or how to feel. I'm not labeling your emotions good or bad, right or wrong. What I am saying is that if you are in distress, then I know what you're feeling is contributing to your unhappiness. You know it, too.

I asked you to question whether your emotions are swaying you or serving you. Where do you put the emotions when they aren't serving you? More importantly, what do you do to prevent them from swaying you in a direction that is counterproductive?

One word: Options.

CHAPTER NINE:

STEP 3. CLARIFY YOUR OPTIONS

Once you've taken time to identify the nature of the problem and gotten some distance from your emotions for a moment, you're ready for Step Three. This is where you identify and clarify your options. Read this next line very carefully.

You ALWAYS have options.

I know it doesn't always feel that way. That's one of the most important reasons that distancing your feelings, though not easy, is essential to problem solving. I have been under the rubble after an emotional earthquake, strangled by betrayal, restrained by fear. I've seen the signs in others and recognized immediately the invisible straitjacket of depression that binds them. They feel powerless. They weren't. You're not. You know that deep down inside. That's why you are reading this book. You know intuitively there's a way out of this difficulty and there are ways to cope while you get to the solution.

In every situation, you're given an opportunity to choose something. There are always at least two choices available to you. Sink or swim, stand or fall, go or stay, right or left, up or down, here or there, better or worse, yes or no, deal or be dealt, bitter or better, over or under, rise or fall, remain or crumble—you have these and more. You can face the problem, or you can avoid it.

I can give you endless examples of the choices people I have worked with have had in all kinds of situations. Like you, they were momentarily blinded by fear or immobilized by hopelessness. Then with some distance from the emotion and using the steps we've discussed, they saw light. Sometimes the alternatives are not clear-cut with one being favorable and the other unfavorable. It isn't always that simple. Often one choice is less painful or less destructive, but you are in charge of the damage control. That can be a victory in a devastating situation. At times the answer is so obvious it doesn't even feel like a choice at all. I'll give you a personal example.

My life was going fine. It was better than fine. I was in a solid marriage. My children were thriving. I had curated the family life that I had missed as a child. I volunteered in the community, serving on several boards of directors for arts and health organizations, and receiving national recognition for my civic fundraising. My husband was in a family business that afforded us a very comfortable upscale lifestyle. I was who I wanted to be and possessed all the things in my early midlife that I thought were the definition of success. I had pulled myself up by my bootstraps and traded them in for Louboutin stilettos.

Then I was blindsided by a crisis I didn't see coming. My husband's family business had suffered a series of major setbacks due to a downward economy. He had worked for months to salvage what he could and to protect me from the reality, but the time came for him to deliver the news that we would have to start over. I immediately went from shock to problem-solving mode. But in the wee hours of the morning in the dark, my mind worked hard to figure out how I could fix the situation. I vacillated between sadness and shock. How could this happen to someone so together? How could I have thought I was in control?

I was in what I call the black hole where despair can make you believe things won't change. Where your soul is shaken and your spirit feels like it's in jeopardy. That you have no choice.

But I knew better. I felt powerless at times but not hopeless. I knew deep down that I could rally and rise.

Why? Not because I was filled with rainbows and lollipops of positivity but because I had done it before.

I had the confidence of resilience.

I dug deep into that problem-solving memory muscle I knew had worked for me before. I evaluated the pile of problems that were on top of me, one by one, and rated their severity to prioritize them. I mentally listed the decisions that were in my power to make. The first was, do I stay in a marriage that had every reason to fail? My trust had been shaken, and admittedly the structure had major cracks, but the foundation was still solid. The love endured. I chose my marriage again.

The second decision was how to keep what was left of the kids' world intact. I knew our priority was them. Everything else could be rebuilt in time, but their need for stability was paramount and immediate. I made keeping myself together a priority so they would have support.

What I chose to do next may surprise you. It certainly seems to me looking back to have been illogical. I returned to college to finish the degree that I had left undone years prior. I needed a job. That would have been the fastest quick fix to help. But something deep inside told me what I really needed was a career. I believe it was a God whisper that said *don't settle in the moment because if you trust yourself you can do far more.* It was my belief from my experiences in my early years that you are as capable as you allow yourself to believe. If I hadn't made that bold choice, I wouldn't have gone back to college and received my master's degree in Counseling Psychology, founded and led a large grief recovery group, and become an entrepreneur. I wouldn't have fed my love of writing and studied the craft so I could become an author. I wouldn't have been prepared to survive the crisis events in my life that would happen during the pandemic. I wouldn't have had the empathy to help others navigate tough times. My calling to help hurting people and write this book happened because of that one choice.

There were many more choices along the way. The choice to move past my resentment and let go of the anger rather than allow them to fester. The choice to resist the temptation to wallow in self-pity or be crushed under the weight of guilt or allow the emotions to consume me. The self-recrimination loomed. Why didn't I see this coming? What could I have done to stop it? What had I done to cause it in some way?

To keep the landslide of blame from taking me down, I grabbed onto my options as lifelines.

As I sat in the dark place, I knew where I wanted to go but had to figure out a route. I could withstand what was happening because I decided early on that some of these choices were "of courses." Of course, I would survive. Of course, I would make sure my kids were okay. Of course, I would stay with the love of my life for the better and for worse that I had promised all those years ago. Of course, we would eventually thrive again. Of course, I would crawl inch by inch out of the very deep and very dark black hole. Of course, when I was in that bleak despair, I vowed that I would give a hand up to anyone else who ever fell into such a place. Of course, I would write this book to be that hand for you.

Those "of course" decisions came from asking myself the questions so I could gain clarity to see my way through. Those are the same questions I'm asking you. Applying the strategies that worked for me will do the same for you. I needed to feel like I had choices.

I did.

So, do you.

Years after my life had crashed and we did achieve total financial recovery, my stoic mother did me the greatest favor. We were talking one day about it all. When I commented that I had done what I had to do because I didn't have a choice. She replied, "Oh, but you did. You could've given up."

I tell you this to remind you that there is no place for humility in survival. There's nothing noble about discounting your bravery when facing a difficulty. Confidence is key. It will sustain you and bolster you when you doubt yourself. Listen to your intuition. You may have to strain to hear that voice deep inside through all the noise around you. Doubt may be the tune stuck in your head repeating loudly. Do all you can to resist it. This is when the positive strategies will help.

Believe.

What if your choices aren't so clear? What if confusion obscures your options? What defines a viable option?

Let's talk about my strategy for discerning what options are available to you. The logical equation would be A (the problem) plus B (what you can do about it—options) equals C (the desired outcome). When you've thought about the problem and the options aren't presenting themselves, I suggest you begin with subtraction instead.

What does that mean?

Okay, think about this next very important strategy. It is a key point of Coping Smart.

Elimination is half of life. You've got to know what you don't want before you can truly know what it is you do want.

What? Yes, you read that correctly. Determining what you don't want to happen or what you don't want to do leads you to determining what you really desire. If you can decide what you definitely do not want, then that option is off the table. You can mark it off the list. Don't spend time spinning your wheels. Get down the road with other possibilities that you determine. Those are all monumental proactive steps forward.

Here's another great coping skill. View your mistakes as an act

of elimination. Haven't you said you'd never do *that* again, referring to a past misstep? If you think of it as a good thing that whatever you did or whomever you brought into your life turned out not to be the best choice, then it's much easier to recoup from the impact. It lessens the burden of regret or self-incrimination. In other words, you won't beat yourself up about it.

Now we come to the word you've probably been expecting me to say. Consequences.

You've heard about consequences your entire life. Consequences were held over your head as a child as punishment. Your teen years were one cautionary tale after another of all the bad things that could happen if you didn't think about the consequences of your actions. Consider the consequences. Face the consequences. Because the act of choosing unwisely is so closely associated with the word, consequences have a negative connotation. (Here's that words matter thing again.) Actually, any action has a consequence. Notice I didn't assign any qualifier. Outcome, result, and impact are all used to define consequence. Those are neutral without a qualifying descriptor. Consequences don't have to be bad. They can be favorable.

This process of clarifying your options is really quite simple.

Now I offer you what I believe is the greatest coping strategy for discerning options in any situation. Four straightforward questions will help you clarify your options and determine your course of action.

- What do you want to do about this situation? Your first instinct is telling you how to react. Your emotions talk the loudest at this initial point.

- What will probably happen if you follow through on that impulse? This is when clarity comes into focus. This is when possible consequences begin to take shape.

Here's my next question. It's the most important question you will ever ask yourself when determining a course of action in a problem situation. I call it *The Litmus Test of Decision Making in Problem Solving.*

- *What's the worst thing that can happen?*

   Think of any and all the consequences of the action you want to choose. Consider who would benefit and who will be collateral damage.

   The final question in this litmus test is the clarifying follow-up. Here's where you determine your action.

- *Can you live with that?*

   If your answer is yes, you can live with the consequences of your decision, then go for it. If your answer is no, then you take that option off the table. This will keep you from making a regrettable mistake in the heat of the moment and clear your mind for more constructive options.

These four questions are an extention of taking time to stop and think in Step One for perspective. In Step Three taking the time to think the process through will reveal the viability of an option and its flaws before you act.

As we've discussed, the less impactful problems like complications and dilemmas will be the most manageable with attitude and perspective as options. Crises require more emotional energy for critical thinking and are more pervasive. Usually they affect most every aspect of your life, as well as your choices, and they involve more people.

Tragedy is the category of problem that holds the greatest risk to your mental and emotional well-being. This is the test of character stuff. I know, you're screaming at this page right now that you've had enough character building to last your lifetime. Enough is enough, right? Well, that's the point. You do have enough. You already possess the character that you need to withstand a tragedy. It's inside you. You have to find ways to tap into it.

Grief is a mighty river. All you see around you is black waters raging and threatening. You know if you allow yourself to fall in, you'll be swept away because you're too exhausted to fight the current.

How do you get over it to the other side?

You build a bridge.

I hear you saying, how on earth do I possibly do that? You can hardly get out of bed much less muster the strength to build a bridge.

Stone by stone.

Look for them. They're everywhere. The little kindnesses you can recognize. The blessings that shine through. The memories that bob up in the endless blackness and provide rest from the constant treading. The people who offer their own experiences and empathy to you against the raging waters. There are successful strategies for finding anchoring rocks to build a bridge to get you over the river of grief. I'll offer those to you in the next chapter.

A tragedy taps and tests every emotional resource.

Denial and acceptance are at opposite ends of the spectrum of choices, with many others in between.

Let's talk about denial in terms of tragedy. It's truly a double edged sword in the way I mentioned earlier. If you cut yourself off from reality in an unhealthy way that keeps you from dealing with the problem and moving forward, or if you avoid dealing with the fallout from a tragedy, then it is truly destructive. It can paralyze your ability to function. It can damage your relationships. It can prevent you from opening yourself to love again because you're afraid to be hurt by loving so much.

Then there's that possibility to use denial as a way to refuse to give up.

Refuse to be denied happiness and recovery.

Refuse to be denied a future past this dark place. Use that edge of the sword to slice deep into the affliction of this pain and amputate the tragedy's ability to steal your life. Grasp and wield that sword. It's in your hands.

In telling you about options for dealing with a tragedy, I must take the opportunity here to let you know that there is no right or wrong way to grieve, as long as it doesn't interfere with your ability to function in any way. You'll find hundreds of books on the subject. Chances are if you have experienced a tragedy in your life, your friends and family members have sent you copies of the latest books to help. I encourage you to find solace and guidance in them, but with a caveat. There are universal stages of grief that can be *possible* and *probable* steps in your recovery process. But they are not all prerequisites or mandates for recovery. Knowing about them and expecting them can prepare you for the rollercoaster ride ahead.

Remember, grief is the byproduct of a problem, and like all problems it's unique to each person it befalls. You may experience all of the stages. You may not. They may come to you in a predictable order. They may not. Well-meaning family and friends may try to tell you how to grieve. They may even lovingly tell you that you're not progressing as they think you should. Don't be concerned about pleasing others or meeting their expectations. Don't feel guilty that you're not "doing the grief thing right."

I was privileged to work with a young couple, Tom and Lucy, after the sudden death of their first baby. During the final weeks of her pregnancy, Lucy went in for a weekly exam and her doctor discovered that there was no fetal heartbeat. The baby had died. The couple had to endure the entire labor process knowing the outcome would be the stillbirth of their infant son. When they came to me for support only weeks later, Lucy voiced her concern that she wasn't grieving properly. We discussed what steps she had taken to begin healing, and how she was coping. It was clear she was earnestly doing everything in her power to get through this heartache. After talking further, she revealed that a close family member told her that she hadn't gone through the stages of grief in proper order. They were concerned that she hadn't been angry. She hadn't been in denial of the reality. And so on. The family member spoke out from a place of love and concern, but without realizing it, they had burdened this grieving young mother with guilt she didn't need or deserve.

My response was to ask Lucy if she had done well in school. As I suspected, she was a straight-A student and top of her law school class. She had gone on to be a high achiever in her career as well. It was clear to me that she was worried about failing at this grieving assignment she had been given. She feared letting herself and those she loved down. I explained to her that grieving has no scoring system. There are no grades given. The only measure of success is whether you can move through it and on to regain a functioning, productive life. I assured her that I believed she was on track to do exactly that. The bonus was she had Tom's complete support and steadfast love. They traveled the road before them, built a mighty bridge across the river of grief, and went on with grace and courage to have three more children and create a beautiful family and life.

It's easy to see that Lucy and Tom could have individually made different decisions with their options. That would have changed the trajectory of their lives and their family. Instead they leaned into each other and chose a perspective that was hopeful and healing.

As a reminder of what we've talked about, perspective is the value you assign any situation. It is the cumulative sum of all the factors and variables that create the lens of your view of the world. These can hinder you or help you cope through a difficulty. They can obscure or reveal your options. Perspective begins to be managed by learning the four ways to discern the nature of a problem. You may *feel* bad, but a bad outcome isn't the only possibility.

I'm going to repeat that for emphasis so that it sinks in and stays in your mind.

You *feel* bad right now, in this moment, but a bad outcome is not the only possible outcome.

Reason and logic are resources to mine for clarity of your options. Analytical thinking is breaking the problem down into digestible parts. See the facts to determine your choices. Then you can think critically about your options to determine your next step. Recovery from any problem comes only through directed intent. This is what problem-solving is; an intentional effort to improve a situation. That's a fancier way to say what you need next is a plan for a workable solution.

It's also the next specific step for Coping Smart.

CHAPTER TEN:

STEP 4. FIND YOUR

WORKABLE SOLUTION

You've gotta have a plan.
—Sue Wentworth Cotton

That's another piece of wisdom from an organic source. I wish I could convey this great quote with the buttery, definitive, southern accent with which it was delivered. My Aunt Sue in all her commonsense wisdom made this declaration around the dinner table one Sunday when the topic of discussion was a wayward young cousin. The other diners were weighing in on his less than prudent behavior and their opinions about the root of his trouble. There was a moment of silence in the conversation. Sue hadn't said much until that moment when she very decidedly declared, "You've gotta have a plan." Then she paused a beat in a perfect moment of timing with command of everyone's attention while we all waited for what was coming next. She followed up with her perfect summation of the young man's problem. "He's got no plan."

There's a recurring theme I recognize with the people who ask me for advice. They want to regain that feeling of having a say, a vote, a sense of management over the difficulty that has them in a place of distress. Drifting aimlessly, wandering in a fog, being tossed about, trapped, weighted down, held back, hands tied, hopeless, helpless—this list of metaphors and similes and adjectives comes from a feeling of loss of control. The idea of that may be more intolerable that the actual problem. You need to get out of this place of uncertainty.

There is no more effective strategy to move forward than to make a plan of action. This plan will be the framework for what I call your workable solution. What does that mean? We've discussed the fact that not all problems are solvable but they are manageable. You decide what will be acceptable to you as a plan of action to overcome the problem. What are you willing to do, to change, to give up, to ask for, to accept, to get to the place that you define as happiness and success?

This process begins with the source of all progress: your thoughts. I know you may have trouble getting your mind to settle enough to think clearly. The thoughts are darting around in your brain, and it's like the proverbial herding of cats. Or, it may be that your mind has shut down into a sluggish pace and the idea of forming a coherent thought sounds overwhelming. I promise you this is where you start your comeback. Make a plan.

Think about your destination.

Where do you want to be? You might say you have no idea. That's okay. Here's a suggestion. How about not here? Let's get you out of this uncomfortable place.

How will you begin? The act of deciding you're ready and open to making a plan is a step of success. You don't have to leave your house, buy anything, or ask anyone what they think or for their help. This step is one hundred percent your call. Even if someone else is part of the problem or could be part of the collateral damage, the plan begins with you.

Every problem can be moved with a plan.

So, let's talk about formulating a plan to find a workable solution to the problem and to cope with the stress it's causing. Some questions will help you find your starting place for this step.

- What action in moving forward is not an option? Mark the things off your list that are beyond your control. This is that act of elimination process that can be applied situationally. There's no point in wasting time and energy. This can often involve the realization that you can't change someone else's behavior. Sometimes you must accept that you can't change certain circumstances. You can only change the direction of your efforts.

- What do you see in the situation that can be moved? Here's where you do get to make a difference.

- What about your behavior can you alter to bring about the change you desire?

- If it's possible, what can you do to influence anyone else involved toward that change?

- Can you be conciliatory or congenial in any way that will move them toward change?

- Are you willing to see that *not now* doesn't mean *not ever*? Think in terms of timing. Pace your expectations. That doesn't mean limit them. It does mean aligning your process with the probable with an eye on the possible.

- Do you see yourself as part of the problem? Here's where you look at the role of mistakes. The sooner you deal with this elephant in the room, the sooner and more successfully you can move forward. You can do that with the same distance you've used for other emotions in the previous chapters. Take shame and blame out of the picture.

Mistakes are those loaded issues that can do more emotional damage than the actual act itself. That's because they come with the incredible aftermath force of guilt. The destructiveness of guilt can't be overstated. It will crush your soul and handicap your ability to trust yourself. Self-condemnation can be so powerful that you can use it to keep you in a destructive relationship or situation. You can convince yourself that you deserve misery because of your mistake. You can choose to turn that around and offer mercy to yourself.

- Could it be that you haven't made a full-fledged mistake? It might have been a misstep. The difference is the measure of the impact. Missteps can be corrected more easily. Don't give into the temptation to catastrophize. Heightened emotion can lead to this very easily. It's part of the reason you did Step Two to identify and clarify the emotions that come up. This relates back to the idea of not giving more drama to a situation than it deserves. If it was indeed a mistake, own it to release it.

- Is a do-over possible? This may entail asking for forgiveness from someone or recalculating you path. Either way you will need to forgive yourself as well and believe you deserve a second chance.

Using the Coping Smart strategies for discerning the nature of the problem you're facing will help you determine your plan for managing it. You've used the strategy to stop and think to identify the severity of the problem. Then you've acknowledged the need to get on top of the emotions that you're feeling. You've clarified your options and considered the consequences. Now it's time to make a plan to find your workable solution. Let's talk about the most workable plan based on the aforementioned four categories of problems.

A COMPLICATION PLAN

These problems are the things that frustrate you. They're everyday stuff. The people in your life that aggravate and irritate you can be complications. The things that happen that conflict with your plans, cause disruption, and unnerve you can gnaw at your contentment. Occasionally the problem may be a constant that you have to manage repeatedly. Complications mainly require a perspective shift. They're almost always in your control as to the outcome or the effect it has on you. You can determine the drama of the moment. The ball is in your court. You can foul out or make a slam dunk. Nail it or get hammered. Pick your favorite phrase that says clear choices to you. Decide how much of yourself you want to give this problem. That means how much time and energy and thought you're willing to devote to it. Is it worth ruining your day or occupying time you could spend on something else more pleasant? You can opt out and not engage in any behavior response at all. That isn't the same as avoiding. Avoidance is the act of turning away without dealing with the problem. When you realize that engaging in conflict is a dead-end that will get you no results, a decision not to engage with someone or in a situation it is an effective coping skill that puts you in charge. Learning to handle complications well is a great confidence builder for the more difficult tasks. You can gain a sense of accomplishment for what you decide not to do.

A DILEMMA PLAN

A dilemma requires an either-or choice. Remember that not all options that come into your mind are favorable. Avoidance or procrastination can be tempting options when you're tired and weary. They feel like the easiest choices. Silence and inaction are forms of acceptance. A dilemma calls for decisive action for a remedy. Remember also that your perspective will determine your action. You're in charge of your response and the outcome. Take it. Use it. Make this work for you. Dial down the drama with decision.

A CRISIS PLAN

This is where consequences will be your best guide. You will have to go all in. You must focus on strategies for management and damage control by carefully thinking through the possible scenarios for each likely outcome as you consider your choices for a course of action. Timing is critical in a crisis. When you use the strategy discussed in Step One—stopping and thinking—in a crisis situation, you give yourself time to assess the problem. However, you don't have the time to procrastinate or the problem will likely escalate. A crisis is also multileveled. It has several moving parts, meaning it requires a great deal of attention often in several directions. A crisis can become life-altering in its scope, but at certain junctures you have a chance to mitigate the impact if and when you act.

A TRAGEDY PLAN

A tragedy is a problem that once set in motion can't be changed. The only variable is your response to the outcome and acceptance or denial of its impact. Grief is the inevitable consequence that you face with a tragedy, and you must be deliberate in your coping strategies or you will be in danger of succumbing to its potential for devastation.

Grief is universal. It happens to everyone multiple times over the course of their life. Working in grief recovery with all age groups and situations, I found that each time it happens in a lifetime, it brings different challenges. Widows and widowers who have had the blessing of long-term marriages find themselves lost in the unfamiliar territory of singleness. Young men and women whose happily-ever-after ends suddenly when their spouse dies unexpectedly. Parents mourn a child and their unfulfilled potential and promise. Brothers and sisters grieve for their siblings they thought would always be there. Children, both young and adult ages, navigate the grief of the end of their first human bond and longest relationship of their lives with the death of a parent.

Physical death isn't the only source of grief. The support group I facilitated was open to anyone grieving any event in life that we call a loss. Broken relationships, whether romantic or friendships, mean the death of a particular vision you have of how your life will be. Emotionally investing in someone else comes with expectations of what that relationship will bring to your life and a promise of reciprocity. When that promise is breached, the place it held in your spirit is now a void. The ache of the emptiness can be a gnawing regret. It's a phantom pain in the now-empty place. That's the essence of grief.

Loss of a job or lifestyle, loss of financial position and stability, health challenges, and divorce all are grieving processes. Something happens without your permission. Your life is altered, and you're left to recover from the impact. I've learned not only about the fragility of life but also the colossal strength of the human spirit. Most valuably, I've learned there is no single correct way to grieve.

Or to recover. You have all of those factors we've talked about that make you the person you are at your disposal to use to find your way. While there is no prerequisite *right way* to grieve, there are two foundational ingredients that I have found grief recovery does require. You will need knowledge and courage. I realize that you aren't feeling very brave at the moment. This problem has you in its grasp, and it seems giving into it is the easiest answer. You're too depleted to fight. I know this feeling. This tragedy is Goliath and all you have is a pebble. What good can that be?

It's everything.

That pebble is the tiny mustard seed of faith that is the power source within you. It's that whisper that says you can do this. It's the spark that offers a glimmer of light against the deep blues of pain. Your very survival is at stake. Now, more than ever, you must make a plan. You need to cross over this river. You need to build that bridge to get to the other side of a tragedy where you can begin to live your life going forward again. This is not as insurmountable as you think. I have specific strategies that have worked for me and for others in dealing with tragedy.

1. THE SAME BOAT STRATEGY

The tragedy in your life feels like you're on *The Titanic*. It's going down, and all you can see is pandemonium. The thought of giving up is scarier than the fate that awaits. You scan the tilting deck and spot a lifeboat about to be lowered. You board the boat and enter the encroaching sea with a few dozen other shocked souls suffering the same uncertainty and fear. Once huddled together waiting to see if you will survive this excruciating situation, you and the others in the boat with you form a bond. You can try to explain it later to someone who wasn't there, but you know that they can't fully comprehend what it was like. Only those who shared that boat, that experience, can know the pain in the same way.

This strategy underscores the benefit of seeking the company of others who are adrift in grief. Shared struggles go a long way to guide your own healing.

As group facilitator, I began the sessions with a request for each person to share what or who they were grieving, when they died, how they died, their relationship to them, and where they saw themselves in their grieving process. Notice I didn't use the word *loss*. It is a loss. However, I always feel a bit uncomfortable using it. It's as if you are saying you did something negligent or careless to cause this suffering. You lose keys or your glasses. Loss is what you feel in the space left behind when a loved one dies. It's a place, not an act. Some say passed or passed away. Some simply say died. Again, no rules here. How you find peace with expressing it, do so.

No one else will experience grief exactly as you do. Additionally, you will experience it differently each time something or someone you love dies. This is why I acknowledged those differences in each group member's story.

When I asked each person to share the circumstance that had brought them to join the group, I discovered the members who were dealing with a physical death were divided into those who had a loved one die suddenly and those who had a loved one die after a prolonged illness. Inevitably, after hearing others' stories, the empathy was palpable. Those for whom the death was sudden each expressed gratitude that their loved one didn't have a prolonged end. They couldn't bear the idea of witnessing that suffering. Their hearts hurt for ones who had. Those for whom the death was protracted over a period of illness spoke openly of their gratitude that they had been given the opportunity to say their good-byes and the other things that might have remained unsaid if they hadn't had the chance. They felt deep sympathy for the ones who didn't get that opportunity. Both groups felt blessed to have their own experience and didn't wish to change places with the others. They were able to see a small blessing they had been given in the shadow of the pain. In that moment, they were also able to come out of that shadow of their individual grief to feel emotion for someone else. That kind of authentic empathy can only come from shared experiences. It is more than a gift you give someone else. It is a balm for an aching soul. Yours and theirs.

Find others who are in this place. The kinship of grief can go a long way toward healing the isolation that comes and lingers. Your experience is yours and unlike any other, but the ways others are finding to cope can be instructional and inspiring. The bond can be a foundational stone in the support pillar for your life going forward.

2. SEEK A SENSEI STRATEGY

Those who have drifted on the river of grief before you and have gotten to the other side hold great wisdom. They are the seasoned soldiers who have a survival story to tell. You need to hear it. You also need to see that survival is possible. They are examples. They don't necessarily have to be people you already know. Widen your circle. Find their narratives and learn from them. Read biographies, attend guest lectures, listen to podcasts. Your library, your place of worship, and community groups are resources available to you. Receive these survival stories and use them to create your own. Their words are your stones to use to build that bridge.

3. THE SKY IS ALWAYS BLUE STRATEGY

The sky is always blue. That's a scientific fact, not wishful thinking. It's only when clouds gather that the beautiful hue is obscured with grayness. Like the clouds that shift and reveal the brilliance behind them, grief can be moved. It takes time. It takes patience.

Wait for it. It requires a degree of acceptance, not for what has happened, but for the belief in your survival. The pain will tug at your brain and the doubt will try to settle in your bones, but if you are patient with yourself, you will find a way across it. Remember that every day is the worst day in someone's life and the best day in someone else's. This is what life is all about. It ebbs and then it flows and ebbs again and so on. Like a lullaby, that's a comfort by divine design. Let the assurance that you will be the one riding the next flow carrying you through the ebb and back again console you. It's your turn for the brighter sky next.

4. THE STARBUCKS LINE STRATEGY

On any given day, in any Starbucks in the world, among the people standing in line are some who are grieving a tragedy. Their pain is silent and secret to the others waiting for their latte and muffin. This is to say that wherever you encounter people, chances are someone's soul is in pain. Someone's heart is bruised or broken. They may be strangers to you. You will never know their story, but it is there standing next to you all the same. This strategy enables you to open yourself to the idea that though you feel like the rest of the world is oblivious to your hurt and they seem happy in their untouched world, the opposite may be true. Rather than viewing that as depressing, think of it as validation that you're not alone, and others are functioning and living their lives despite the burden. You can too. You feel invisible. You feel like the only hurting person on a happy planet. Those are imposter emotions that beg for your surrender. They threaten to undermine your inner will to survive. Many other people are stalled on the road where you are right now. Understanding that goes a long way in healing the bitterness and disappointment of grief.

5. THE GIFT STRATEGY

Stay with me here. This isn't some empty phrase to consider in a time when you don't have the patience or the strength. I promise you with time and intent you can believe it and use it to lift you from the overwhelming despair of grief. Even if you can't be all in right now, I urge you to consider the possibility as time goes on in your journey.

In every tragedy there's a gift of sorts.

Dig deep for it. It's there. You might have been flattened by the blows of a tragedy. You might think you'll die from it. You're face down on the ground. You have no strength to resist the gravity to pull yourself up. But you will. You will sit up, crawl, then stand, then walk again unbent. And therein lies the gift. You will know for certain you can survive. It is the major support beam of resilience on your blueprint. You'll have confidence that the structure you're building is strong. That's your gift. You will be a visible affirmation for someone else when they are facing a tragedy. Then, you will be their gift.

I must say here that I do not subscribe to the theory that you can find closure in grief. Ever. A loss leaves a hole in your soul. Period. That void can't be closed but it can be filled. But it takes time. Moving through the sludge of grief is tedious and tiring. Understanding and accepting that time is the only measure that matters to begin healing will help. Slowly you can find solace in what life offers you as comfort; interests, places, and people and you can allow them to fill that emptiness.

Your Advisory Board

This strategy can really set your workable solution plan in motion. Form an advisory board for support. This is a creative way to find mentors and motivation. There are people you know whose advice you trust. There are those who inspire you. There's someone you can name whom you respect for the way they conduct their life professionally and personally. Make a list.

The people you choose can be different ages and in different phases of life. They can be similar to each other and to you or they can be opposite. They need not know each other. You will find those around you have much to offer and will usually be more than happy to help especially when you let them know you are looking to them as mentors you trust.

Don't feel comfortable asking people to be on your board? Don't think you know anyone to fill a seat? The really exciting part is that they don't have to be someone you actually know or will ever know. You can create this group like you would a fantasy sports team. You can pick a business titan, a well-known spiritual leader, a favorite celebrity, a world-class athlete, a wellness guru, a best-selling author, or even your favorite musician whose work moves you. Choose anyone you admire. Read everything you can and glean gems from their quotes. Use that to inform you and to lift you.

I give credit for this brilliant strategy to a famous entrepreneur I know well. It was during a time I was at a very low point and was searching for a path out. He gave me this idea while offering to be the first member of my board and suggested I gather others around me to support me in my quest to recover from a major crisis in my life. I chose a handful of people to seek out for advice. Some knew me and others did not, but those who didn't had talent and wisdom I needed, so I silently designated them as members in my mind as I sought out their expertise. It became a coping strategy for me.

You'll find the act of doing this will reveal all sorts of resources, some that you might not have discovered otherwise. Get creative, explore the possibilities, and network anywhere with anyone you can think of that might have answers for you. Once you add someone, mine their connections and associates for suggestions. This can be invaluable. These individuals can be angels, and you may find yourself amazed that one single connection can change your life. *Leave no stone unturned* is a very valuable piece of advice. Consider a few things when you begin to think about this strategy:

- What about you is something that you recognize isn't your strongest skill? This is my way of not using the word *weakness*; I know you're feeling weak in the coping department right now and the last thing you need is another negative term to apply to yourself or your situation. So, let's call it a desired skill set.

- Who do you know or know of who possesses this skill in full? This is someone you should definitely consider for your advisory board. You need what they've got. Now get it for yourself with their help.

- What professional assistance do you need for the problem? If it's legal then find an attorney. If it's financial then find an accountant, banker, or broker. If it's spiritual then find a religious or spiritual leader. If it's particular to your job or industry, then find a consultant or mentor. If it's psychological then find a therapist, psychiatrist, counselor, or coach. If its physical find a medical doctor, nurse practitioner, physical therapist, acupuncturist, aromatherapist, chiropractor, or reiki master.

- Choose one friend. You might have a large group of friends to choose from, but I urge you to choose carefully. This should be *the* friend you know always has your best interests, foremost, regardless of where they are in their own life. They hurt for you when you hurt, but love you enough to tell you when you are slipping into self-pity quicksand. They don't tire of your weariness but carry you when you need it. They are the same ones who are thrilled for your good fortune and celebrate you without reserve or jealousy. I saw an interview with Oprah Winfrey once where she was recounting a conversation that she had with her long-time partner Stedman Graham. She was saying she had realized she had done something that she later thought made her look foolish. She was lamenting her surprise that no one in her entourage had stepped up to tell her that she was embarrassing herself. Stedman's reply explains what I'm talking about in choosing which of your associates and friends to trust when you need them most. He told Oprah that what she needed was someone who would tell her the truth. Many of the good people around her had their own agenda for keeping her happy and feeling good about herself. It may be they meant no harm but wanted to keep her happy at any cost.

You need a heart you can trust.

If you're looking for a member for your board, count me in. Once you have your board, your fantasy team, or a combination of both in place it will help you feel less isolated, less lost, and more supported. Let it lift you.

Begin to formulate your plan. You've heard about *doing the work* that it takes to get to a place of emotional well-being. Don't think of it as work. Think of it as action. Make a list of pros and cons. Put it on a spreadsheet. Think it through. Make a flow chart of action. Design a vision board. Write an outline. Sketch it out. Make it real. Set it in motion in your mind and then on paper if that helps. Tell it to someone. Enlist their support. Encourage their feedback. Listen to their advice. The relief will begin in knowing you are mentally moving in the right direction even before you do anything else.

But what about the stress that the problem has caused? What about the new stress that may arise from making these steps forward? You may have a new sense of anxiety about the plan working or new doubt plaguing your best intentions.

Let's get you out from under that stress.

CHAPTER ELEVEN:

STEP 5. THE 7 R'S OF COPING

Everything we've talked about so far is a component of Coping Smart. Everything you've said, every question you've answered, every thought you've formulated, every decision you've made, every aha moment you've had have all informed you and are directing you toward success. From the first moment you opened this book, you've been Coping Smart.

I'm really excited for you. Now you know you've got to have a plan. Hopefully you've already begun to make it. This is huge progress. Now let's talk about what happens next. I'm a mega fan of preparedness. I can't overemphasize to you the paramount importance of planning for what you'll do when your plan needs support. The secret to being prepared is the realization that even when you think you've thought of everything, something will come up you didn't expect. That doesn't always mean something negative. It simply means something you might not have anticipated.

Let me tell you one thing to plan on for sure. Once you begin to move forward, your pace will vary from day to day. At first, you may take off rolling, and before you know it you've really gotten down the road a good distance. Sometimes you'll encounter other drivers, the people in your life who get in your way or slow you down. Some try to cut you off or get in your lane and try to force you aside. Then there will be days or weeks that you are at a standstill in the traffic crowding around you. It's tough to sit and idle when you're ready to blast off. Impatience can be unbearable and destructive.

Think in terms of building from a blueprint. Weather happens and slows your progress. You have to wait until certain craftsmen or materials are available. Hurry up and wait are a theme in construction.

If you know this will happen, then you won't be blindsided. Anticipation is a good thing. Not to be confused with the intrusive or even catastrophic anticipation that causes anxiety, *informed* anticipation is preparedness and good planning. Think in terms of expectations. Set realistic expectations.

You can implement support strategies during the times your momentum gets slowed down or you get distracted by the unchanging landscape around you. This is to say, what you need and will continue to need is effective ways to cope while you travel this road.

This is the relief I've mentioned that I know you're seeking. You want the discomfort of the problem in your life to ease up. The anxiety has ramped up and you can't think clearly. You can't sleep. You can't stop the roar in your head. The depression is closing in, and you're shutting down. You need the positivity you're practicing so faithfully to support you in measurable ways to combat the negative thoughts that persist. Whether the number on the pain management scale is a one or off the charts past ten, you want it to feel better. The ultimate goal is for it to go away. You've been knocked off balance. It feels like the world is upside-down or at least like you need to steady yourself from the blow. What you crave is emotional equilibrium. You're going to need some specific steps to get you there.

Sometimes the discomfort of a problem is so intense that you want a quick fix. It's tempting to self-medicate and self-soothe with prescription drugs, alcohol, sex, gambling, and other obsessive behaviors. When looking for ways to cope through a problem situation, you must not cop out with destructive behavior. This is rubber meets the road time in your journey. Don't compound your troubles with unfavorable decisions. Save yourself with intentional effort for the long haul instead of numbing the temporary pain with behavior that has potentially permanent side effects.

As a member of your advisory board, I offer you seven successful strategies to use as Coping Smart techniques to cope through the difficulty in your life and get out from under the stress. I call them **The 7 R'S of Coping**.

1. REFRAME

You can't stop thoughts from coming into your head. But you can change them. Find a different way to think about the problem. Think of your cell phone camera. Change the view. Find a better angle. Focus. Use a filter for a better shot. Because visuals help, think of the problem you're experiencing literally as a canvas in a frame. It can look very different in a rustic barnwood frame than it does in Baroque gold gilt. You can make it more appealing, give it more import, or tone down its effect with the way you display it. Get creative. Design a new frame to make the situation more acceptable. You're going to think *something*. You're going to feel *something*. It might as well be something good.

Let me give you some examples. You've been let go from your job. You're devastated and angry. That's expected. Once you've tired of feeling lousy you can reframe it as the opportunity to find a better position with a more desirable company with room for advancement. You may have been overlooked at your present job and didn't receive the promotion you wanted. You resent the person who got the position, and your boss for overlooking you. Okay, that's normal. Then you can reframe it as a signal that it's time to make yourself indispensable so that you are the choice for the next and more upper-level placement. Your offer on the house you wanted to buy was turned down and you're overwhelmed with disappointment. Then you realize that you're positioned and already loan approved and ready to perform when the more perfect house comes on the market.

A similar thing happened to Cameron and Adam. They needed a larger house because their family had outgrown their starter. They had high hopes of getting into a particular neighborhood. They put their house on the market and sold it within days. The contract stipulated they had to vacate immediately. That put them in a bind to find a new one. The market was favorable for sellers but not for buyers, which meant they had sold at a great price on their property, but they had to settle for a neighborhood next to the more desirable one they wanted because of their budget constraints. They could have thought they made a mistake by not waiting until the market changed and let their disappointment overshadow the excitement of a new home for their growing family. Instead, they reframed the picture of their perfect house in their minds and decided to concentrate on their good fortune in getting money from their sale by reinvesting it to buy one of only a couple of new construction houses in the older neighborhood they could afford. Fast forward eight years. The neighborhood they could have felt they settled for became the new hotspot for tear-down and rebuilds. In that short time frame they not only now live in a fabulous area, they doubled their money.

If the problem is a matter of a breakup of a relationship, here's where I tell you something you've heard before. If someone you love has left you, then you have a choice to think of it as the worst thing that could have happened, or you can reframe that picture in your mind. Instead of seeing yourself standing alone, look at the space beside you as room for the right person you might have missed if the other had stayed.

I had a client who purchased an actual picture frame to use for this purpose. Like most new frames it came packaged with a sheet of paper in it with a photo of a random attractive model. The picture was of a guy who was actually her preferred physical type; dark haired and blue eyed. Instead of removing it, she left the mock photo in and looked at it every day as a way of saying, *this time in my life is temporary and someone else just right for me is waiting to be in my frame*. It didn't bring that exact person into her life. What it did was put her into a posture of openness so that she didn't check out in her misery and miss what was possible next.

Reframing is a positive mind game to master. This doesn't mean pretending. It doesn't mean deluding yourself into an unhealthy mental state. It simply means putting a new favorable spin on a situation to cope through it. Think of it in terms of selling an idea. It's like advertising for what you want. Something I do to find a new way to think about a problem situation I'm in is to think of it as a movie, and I'm writing a tagline for the trailer ad. The tagline sets up the premise of the story with a provocative hint of what the outcome may be. It's intriguing enough to consider the possibilities.

The anatomy of any story is someone is living in their ordinary world, then a precipitating event creates a predicament for them that incites and moves them to action, which puts them at risk of losing everything, but then they take action that produces a wanted outcome. Why does the screenwriter put the lead character at risk? Because that's the anatomy of life. That's your life and mine. That's pretty cut and dry, but it's actually the way stories are structured. Think about your favorite movies. Don't they follow a similar formula?

I know you're saying, okay that's fiction and the stories aren't real. I assure you all fiction is based on reality. It may be bits and pieces from real life mixed with imagination, but imagination is built on what you know. Stories are truths, even if the names are changed to protect the guilty. Isn't that why you watch movies? You see a predicament you relate to and are moved to take the ride with the characters to see it through to a good ending. It gives you hope for your own life.

There are a handful of premises that are the result of a handful of universal human emotions, but there are millions of ways to tell the story. That's why the same plot never gets old when told in a new way. Think of some more of your favorite books or movies. Can you see any that are on the same theme? Along the way, there's a problem that threatens to destroy the characters' lives until they come up with a way to turn it around. The clever author finds a new way for the characters to think and behave to solve the problem.

Happy endings begin with reframing a sad tale.

You're in the middle of your life story. You're the author of what happens. The sooner you grasp this fabulous revelation, the sooner you are on your way to building the life you want. You are the architect.

You can reframe and rename your emotions to change the story of this problem. Those emotions can be dynamite that is capable of blowing up your life or fireworks to light up the night sky. It's all in your hands. You get to choose. You see it through your lens. Remember the lenses are interchangeable. You may not make the situation, but you make the decision of how it plays out. How that happens depends on you and the nature of the relationship.

I have a creative strategy for reframing that I developed to use with the other kinds of relationship problems. You probably have a relative or someone that is inextricable from your life. You can't terminate the relationship, and you are forced to deal with them on a regular basis. This could be a blood relative and part of your family legacy. They may be an in-law, or as my sister-in-law refers to these marriage relations, "out-laws." It could be a friend of your partner's that is in their life and in yours by association. It could be a neighbor, your boss, or a work associate who's in your life to stay. Even though these people are in your life in an unavoidable way, you have a choice to allow the strain of the relationship to cause you stress or learn to ease the distress of having to interact with them. If you don't, these types of relationships can have pervasive and corrosive effects.

If the problem you're having is due to one of these relationships, then I suggest you sit down and consider this. What you would say if you were asked to write their obituary? Okay, hang with me here. I'm not suggesting hurtful negative thinking or wishing harm on anyone. It's the opposite. This is a way to search for the good in someone. Think long and hard about this. In writing an obit you have to concentrate on the desirable aspects of someone's personality to present them in a positive light. This is say something nice or don't say anything time. You recount their kindnesses or at least their more favorable moments. You'll be amazed when you take the time to search for the good, you'll probably find some. They haven't shown you much of their good side so you may have to search. Locate it. Mark it on your map.

Maybe your mother-in-law never misses a chance to take a passive-aggressive insult shot at your clothes, your home furnishing choices, and your weight, but she adores your children. Your boss is a relentless taskmaster who has no concept of boundaries, expects you to work holidays and weekends without complaint, suffers no fools, but anonymously pays tuition for several underprivileged students. That friend of your partner's is a bit of a user who doesn't show any appreciation and has no respect for boundaries, but they are devoted to their special-needs sibling. That surly neighbor never says a kind word to anyone, but cares for every stray that comes into the neighborhood. Your dad rarely shows you affection, is seldom satisfied, but he never says no when you need him to say yes. It doesn't mean you cut them slack for how they have treated you, but you can pass them with greater ease on your way forward rather than allow them to be roadblocks.

Do you see how reframing the picture you're in can give it a new and more appealing look? Isn't the effort to create a new view worth the peace of relief it can bring?

2. RESIST

Resist the temptation to ruminate. Focus on the moment. This way you can keep your thoughts from drifting to the side of the road and into a ditch. Replaying the should haves, could haves, and would haves steer you head-on into a wreck. They can spin you around and leave you pointed opposite of where you want to go. You can get stuck there broken down and unable to move forward. Distract yourself. This is a good place to kick in some constructive denial in the form of refusing to go there. You may even find it helpful to use a physical activity to get your mind going in the direction you desire. Walk it off. Run. Bike. Go to spin class or yoga. Take back your mind. Don't let the negative thoughts prevail. Read a book. Watch a movie. Craft or build something. Music is another great distraction. It is also a great mood stabilizer.

3. REPLACE

Thoughts flood your mind the same way blood flows in your veins and air fills your lungs. It is automatic and involuntary. You may think it's that definitive, but it's far from it. Unlike the other involuntary functions of your body, you can control your thoughts once they manifest. Intrusive thoughts are particularly stubborn in their persistence and resistance to being avoided. They can easily magnify into catastrophic thinking, and before you know it you've fallen down the rabbit hole of impending disaster. When an intrusive thought comes and brings those negative feelings that stress and distress and depress you, then they must be replaced to mitigate their effect. Here's where you can get creative again. Just as your imagination can run wild with worst-case scenarios you can use it to create a constructive scene where you prevail. Go further and build a worthy fantasy. Write

164

the story your way. Your mind believes what you tell yourself when you say it enough.

4. RATE

This problem has you feeling anxious. It may have you feeling depressed. Both are adverse effects from stress. Examining and quantifying their effects will give perspective on how to manage them. Give it a number from one to ten. This is a quantitative rating tool that physicians use to help their patients rate physical pain. Like rating the severity of a problem, rating the pervasiveness of anxiety and depression will give you a feeling of control and a chance to distance. The act of being analytical in your assessment will give you that. Make it more clinical in your approach than emotional. Assigning a number to the intensity will go a long way to manage it. Then, most importantly, you can also monitor your progress as the number decreases.

5. RECALL

This may sound counterintuitive. I've recommended that you not ruminate, so why am I asking you to recall the past? The difference is, I'm suggesting you remember and concentrate on the past successes in your life.

When did you take charge and succeed?

When did you choose action over inaction?

When did you say enough is enough?

When did you resist self-pity and choose self-reliance?

What decisions have you made that put you on the road to success?

When have you conquered fear?

What did you do to triumph in the face of failure?

What failure did you turn around into a victory?

Recall your brilliant decisions and actions. You did it before. You can do it again.

6. REVEL

Take any and every opportunity to celebrate. I realize that celebrate sounds like a large reaction when the positive event may be small. I also realize that you may not be able to even fathom such an overtly positive act. But here's your chance to take back your power and begin to turn the problem around.

Every tiny step forward is a victory.

Every situation you reframe.

Every deal-breaker you define.

Every boundary you put in place.

Every unpleasant memory you resist.

Every intrusive thought you replace.

Every time you rate and quantify stress and anxiety and their effect in order to mitigate them.

Every past success you recall.

These are all worthy of celebrating. What does celebrating do to you emotionally? It puts you in a positive and hopeful state of mind. It brings joy into your brain releasing dopamine, serotonin, oxytocin, and endorphins that naturally stimulate your body and mind. Stress subsides and happiness flows. It is a tangible, measurable, quantifiable, actual act of personal development toward happiness.

7. REST

Depending on the category of problem in your life, the degree of weariness that accompanies emotional distress can vary widely. Maybe you're simply tired of thinking about it. Perhaps you're exasperated that it occupies so much of your mental time. It may be more dramatic. You're exhausted. The thoughts roll around and bump into each other in your brain non-stop, but you can hardly capture one to put a coherent thought together. You're bone-tired, but sleep eludes you as the negative thoughts take over and hold you hostage. The best coping strategy is to find a way to rest. Sleep is a biological need. Rest is the emotional equivalent. It is a calming, a dialing down of the stress and all the side effects of that toxicity. You are the only one who can do it.

Think of it as the counterpart to hydration. You know the importance and essentialness of keeping your body hydrated. When you are thirsty, you quickly act. When you get that signal headache that warns you that your water level needs replenishing, you don't think twice about drinking water as a remedy. In fact, you probably keep a water bottle on you most of the time. You know that if you ignore your thirst and these signs of distress, the consequences can be life-threatening. The same should happen when your mind signals it's fatigued.

Emotional overload can cause mental confusion and a hypersensitivity to stress. You become easily agitated and overreact to negative stimuli. Everything irritates you. Everyone gets on your nerves. Just as your body is in danger of shutting down when it needs water, your mind does the same when it needs a time of respite to recover and reset.

These strategies will give you a feeling of doing something about a situation that may otherwise feel out of your control. That can be a huge accomplishment. Doing anything feels monumental when you're in distress. Use that as an incentive to make a move forward rather than a reason to shut down. Each strategy is simple in concept and requires only your attention and focus in the moment. No subscription is required. No prescription is necessary. No membership to join. There is no financial commitment. This is about your emotional investments.

This is Coping Smart.

You owe it to yourself to manage the stress. The important people in your life deserve it. You can do this. You can take charge of your emotions, your thoughts, and your perspective and make them work for you instead of against you. These strategies aren't dependent on anyone else's agreement or cooperation.

You only need you.

Think of all the times you've clicked the Agreement to Terms call to action on websites you visit. Before you can buy that item or subscribe to that service you want, you're required to comply with specific policies. Make these strategies your guidelines to coping through the stress of waiting for your workable solution. Then get in agreement with yourself.

Let's put the imagery back to the road you're traveling. It's pouring down rain and your visibility of the road ahead is low. Use your headlights. Turn your windshield wipers on high. The rain may make the trip tougher and more stressful, but it won't stop you if you use the resources that are available to you. Straight ahead remains the same direction no matter the surrounding conditions.

The key is to keep moving. Keep going forward in your mind. The view may change, your visibility may be challenged, but the road is still ahead to get you where you want to go. Keep driving. You'll get there.

LET'S TALK ABOUT WHAT'S NEXT

CHAPTER TWELVE:

FREEDOM

Now you've gotten clarity and a plan you may still feel something holding you back. Let's talk about the "why" question again because I know how hard it is to grasp the idea that there may be no answers. You need to know why. Why did this problem happen to you? Why do you always end up with the short end of the stick? Why doesn't that person love you? Why do your best efforts not pay off? Why does someone who is a terrible person seem to have it all, and you are suffering? Why don't the good guys always win, and the bad guys always lose? Why does an innocent child get cancer? Why do good people die before they have time to change the world? Why don't people just do the right thing? Why weren't you chosen instead of that person who isn't as deserving? Why don't they see what you're going though? Why can't they change? Why can't they just be happy? Why did they take their own life? Why did a pandemic happen?

There's no end to all the questions and no beginning for all the answers. Sometimes there is no clear answer to why. So much agony comes from questioning the unanswerable. Sitting across from hurting souls, I have come to understand the inadequacy of our ability to understand these questions.

I've wrestled with the whys in my life until I was exhausted. I was also disgusted, indignant, resentful, incredulous, jaded, cynical, wounded, confused, confounded, heartsick, dejected, discouraged, crestfallen, and unsatisfied. I want to spare you that time, effort, and pain. Some answers will never be revealed to you. At least while you are here on earth.

What is known is that you can move past the need to know why if you try. My mantra is this:

Let *next* be the antidote to *why*.

Find what you can do if you keep hitting the wall of *can't*. This is the core of my methodology, my modality, my philosophy, my strategy, my ethos, my ideology, my code. Do something that moves you forward. You can't go wrong by pursuing what's next. Remember, forward has multiple directions as well. You can take a step forward that is to the left or right, east or west. Go has options. But realize, you must move past the why. The why is the fallen tree limb across your road. You might be able to drag it out of the way yourself with enough effort, or you may need a little help from someone. The why might be a downed powerline in your way. You know as long as it's live it can do more damage. It's the flooded intersection. Whatever shape you give it in your mind you must also form an action to move it. You want the freedom of the open road without anything to stop you. There's the optimum word.

Freedom.

Doesn't that sound divine?

To be free from worry and anxiety and stress.

Let's talk more about how very much you are in control even if you don't feel it or see it. I'm going to use a fictional story that you know well to illustrate some points here. I am using fiction because sometimes it's hard to relate to someone's predicament if it isn't the same as yours. It's easy to dismiss it if they aren't on the same age or in the same financial position, or they don't do something they way you would or have. You say things like, yeah but... they don't have it as bad as I do...they don't have my bills to pay... they don't have four kids to support… their fiancé didn't break up with them with a text…their wife didn't leave them for the soccer coach… they didn't work their tail off to have the promotion go to that sleazy guy… they didn't have to deal with the sexual harassment… they weren't bullied as badly as I was… on and on. As I mentioned before, a story of any kind, whether reality or myth, follows a pattern. That's because human behavior follows patterns. You recognize them when you see them. That's why they're appealing. You understand the emotions because you've had them all. However, you've probably never analyzed a fictional story as a problem to be solved. It may be way closer to your own than you think.

Dorothy in *The Wizard of Oz* is a great example to think about. Don't groan. I know it gets overused a lot. That's because so many people of all ages know the story and because of its perfectly relatable message. But, I'm going to ask you to look at it in a whole new way. It's not about the *no place like home* stuff. She's lost. You get that. She goes through every possible obstacle to get back home. You get that because that's where you are, finding your way out of a situation and back to the place in your life before the problem came along. This is a story about mistakes.

Dorothy screwed up.

Dorothy is going about her everyday life living on the farm. She loves her aunt and uncle, makes friends with the farmhands, dreams of rainbows and bluebirds, and loves her little dog. That's her ordinary world. Then it gets rocked in a way she didn't see coming. She has feelings that take over, and she reacts in an emotional response.

Mistake 1

When Dorothy's dog Toto causes trouble, mean old Almira Gulch takes him away from Dorothy. Feeling sad and resentful that her aunt and uncle won't help her, she decides to run away from home.

That knee-jerk decision leads to her getting swept up in the tornado that rips through the farmland.

Mistake 2

In her desire to get away, Dorothy ends up in the flying house that lands on and accidentally kills The Wicked Witch of the East, setting off a domino chain of disastrous events. The Wicked Witch of the West turns on her unfairly and alters the course of her life.

Okay. Let's stop for a moment and look at this example story so far. Dorothy is going about her life, then something happened. The precipitating event of Mrs. Gulch taking Dorothy's dog incites what happens next. Dorothy's reactions to the problem and its stress results in her having two more problems on her hands. One she set into motion when her emotional reaction to a problem got the best of her. She didn't stop to think about her options or the consequences, so her reaction was not the best choice. The other screw-up, the house Dorothy was in during the tornado landing on and killing the witch, was fate. What exactly is fate? You hear that word a lot when people talk about problems. They use it when they mean a problem couldn't be helped or avoided. You can hear the *tisk tisk* of pity in their tone. Too bad that bad thing happened rings in their lament.

I think fate's another word you can spin for your benefit or use as an excuse for letting life happen to you without choosing a favorable rebuttal. Fate can befall you or it can benefit you. This is that perspective thing again. You choose the view. See how all of this works together all the way through a problem? Keep with me here because there's more.

I like the word *destiny*. It has a more hopeful connotation that what happens next is of good benefit. Fate sounds ominous. Destiny is a designated promise. Either way the idea is that what happens, the problem, is somehow predetermined. Again, you can view that as hopelessly inevitable and beyond your control, or as incredibly hopeful and yours to use. The problem can be that wrong turn we talked about earlier that can lead to the right road. The problem has to happen for your ultimate good.

Back to the story. Now Dorothy has to find a way out of Munchkinland and home again. She's on a quest. Here we have the metaphoric Yellow Brick Road. To get to where she wants to go, Dorothy has to choose a direction. The big message here is she can't go forward toward home without moving. Staying stuck there is an option she can't entertain if she wants to get home. Listen very closely to this next part of the story. Dorothy encounters other people on the road along the way who offer their companionship and their counsel. Each of them gets pulled into her story by association. The Wicked Witch of the West threatens the Scarecrow by wielding fire his way only because he's with Dorothy. The Tin Man almost completely rusts, and the Cowardly Lion is nearly scared to death, all because they are part of the tailspin of Dorothy's story. See the connection? Now they each have a problem. Sometimes the story is yours and sometimes you're part of someone else's. This is important to grasp. Determine why you are where you are in order to discern your course of action.

The group bands together, makes a plan, overcomes some obstacles reaching Oz with the hope they have found their answer, only to be told they must conquer what they all fear most before their wishes are granted. You know that feeling. You think you've figured it out, and then there's a setback. Dorothy did the things you've done or are doing. She cried some. She was depressed. She was scared. She was anxious. She was indignant. She got mad.

You know all of the obstacles Dorothy meets along the way. Take a moment to relate them to your journey. What are your flying monkeys, angry apple-throwing trees, sleep-inducing poppies, scary castle guards? How can you vanquish the Wicked Witch of a problem you're facing? Has a wizard in your life disappointed you by not being what they seemed and promised you something they can't or don't deliver?

There are lots of lessons here. Dorothy had a problem and she didn't take the time to stop and think to analyze the situation. She acted impulsively when her emotions get the best of her. She makes mistakes.

Then she realizes she has to overcome this problem to move forward. She does what we've talked about. She refuses to dwell on why this happened to her. She doesn't get stuck on blaming herself or anyone else for the trouble that she was in. She weighs her options and makes a plan. She follows through bolstered by her unwavering belief that she can. She faces the roadblocks and overcomes them to find her way back home.

Of course, you're familiar with the ending when Glenda the Good Witch informs Dorothy that she had the power to go home all along. Every time I watch the movie, I'm astounded that Dorothy takes this news so well. She could have said, *are you kidding me?* Why did she have to go through all of that? And what about those magical shoes? Everybody thought the shoes were the answer.

The real solution was in Dorothy's inner strength. Her ability to look at the problem and meet it head on. Her perspective to see the problem as a challenge to be met with her resourcefulness. Her resistance to self-condemnation over her mistakes. Her willingness to move forward. Her resilience to defeat. Her empathy for others, even when she was in the middle of her own distress. Her refusal to be denied what she thought she deserved. Her insight into the purpose of it all.

Dorothy was her own best solution. She made it work for her. It had nothing to do with the damn shoes and everything to do with her. The only magic you need is the magic within you. That wondrous part of you that says *yes* to the noes, and *what's next* to the whys, and *just watch me* to the no ways.

We have to take a moment to talk more about mistakes. I have a personal note here. Whenever I have made a mistake, I find myself in a wrestling match with my soul. I can take a lot of what life shovels out. I have trouble with the stuff I shovel onto myself. When I do something ill-advised (which is a generous way of saying something I do that is stupid), I have to resist the temptation to beat myself to an emotional pulp. This is a great way to get sidetracked from the situation at hand. You've got to pass the past when you realize you've made a mistake and keep going until it's out of sight. It's done, but you're not. The recognition of your participation is the first step out of the mess you've stepped in so that you can clean it up and move forward.

The hardest part of moving forward with your plan may be the part you hear about in every piece of self-help advice.

Let it go.

Heard that before? Sounds great, but how do you do that?

You have already used these strategies earlier. They will serve you here as well.

- Recognize the *whys* that you know. Those things you've acknowledged about yourself and the situation.

- Turn the *whys* into *wisdom* to move you forward.

- Leave the unanswered *whys* behind you as you go. Think of it as emotional ergonomics.

Make moving forward more efficient by carrying less with you.

Whew. That's so tough. This requires what may well be the most of anyone's humanity.

Forgiveness.

Forgiveness will set you free. That's no exaggeration. Oftentimes you must forgive yourself first. You made a mistake. It may have been reckless or incredibly stupid. It might have been devastatingly destructive. Then the soul thieves come into play. Resentment and regret are powerful emotional forces that can eat you alive if left unchecked. They will chip away at your confidence to trust yourself. The pain is chronic and residual. Once you gain clarity to see the part you played in the situation you can redeem yourself with finding a workable solution.

Save yourself. Then you are your hero. You'll have that to stand on.

So you screwed up.

Forgive yourself and learn from it.

Then there's the forgiveness you're required to give others who have hurt you. This is deep in your spirit work. It is work. You already know that I don't like to use that terminology in what I do in helping people because of that word thing again. Work has a negative meaning to most people. It means putting out more effort than you really want to extend. It's about having to, requirements, exhausting stuff. That's the last thing you want to think about.

Instead of thinking of it as doing the work here, let's call it finding your energy source. Take a moment to reframe like you've learn to do in these chapters. Let's go back to the dark place metaphor. You're feeling your way down the black hall of blame. You're patting the wall in search of a light switch. Voila! You make the light come on. You initiate the healing with your intentional action.

You will not go as far on the road as you could if you don't forgive.

Think of forgiveness as the solvent you need to loosen the grip that unforgiveness has on you. Then you can release yourself. This is the letting go part.

Forgiveness doesn't require amnesia. You don't need to forget. In fact, I recommend remembering what someone has done that caused you pain so you will see it coming next time and stop it. Reframe it as well. Think of it differently than as a measurement of pain. Try a measurement of distance from the difficulty as a marker to note. Distance yourself from the resentment. Remember it in a way that says to your mind: *Good to know. I'll remember that for next time.* Better yet, use it to make sure there isn't a next time. You can spare yourself with knowledge. The trick is to remember in a way that *feels* like valuable information. Call up the emotions you feel when you are equipped with the knowledge you need to proceed with confidence. It is invaluable for your personal growth. Let's talk about some questions to ask.

- Do you have someone to forgive in this situation?

- Can you see the ways that has held you back and kept you from moving forward?

- Does the person recognize the part they played in your unhappiness?

- Can you release your need to have them acknowledge their role?

- Is being right worth more than being at peace?

- Can you let go of the resentment you feel?

- Are you the one you need to forgive?

- Will you cut yourself the slack to be forgiven?

- Is holding on to the self-condemnation worth the discomfort?

- Can you see regret as self-punishment that is optional?

- What is freedom from the emotional toll of resentment and regret worth?

Also I want to remind you that it's okay to have days you don't feel up to par. With experts telling you to be grateful and to use gratitude as positivity motivation, you may have guilt when you stop to consider the pain others are experiencing. So many people have it worse you tell yourself. Who are you to moan and complain? Please remember to use gratitude as a powerful coping skill, not as a scorecard.

Now I give you the word you've heard me say several times before because it is so important to your success in this endeavor to overcome a problem and get back on track. I hope you'll keep it close when resentment and regret creep into your heart as you're searching your soul for forgiveness.

Mercy.

What a glorious word. What a miraculous gift available to you to bestow to someone else, or better still, to yourself. To show mercy is to pardon. To pardon is to acknowledge but with the bonus of release. To release is to give one freedom. It's the get out of jail card. Show mercy to those who have hurt you and to yourself. The feeling of freedom will astound you.

CHAPTER THIRTEEN:

RESILIENCE

When you're feeling raw from a difficulty, you question why it's so uncomfortable. Why is this pain so powerful in your life? You also wonder why some people handle problems better than others. How do they do it? Why don't problems rattle them the way they rattle you? Were they born with a natural resistance to stress? Why can't you cope well? Is this stress part of your legacy, or your wiring, or your experiences, or the way you've handled relationships?

Some people stay calm in the storm. Some rally after being slammed to the floor by tragedy and find a way to thrive. Some are like that inflatable child's toy that you can punch and punch, and it rebounds back upright. What is that?

This is the most potent superpower of the human soul.

Resilience.

Like all human attributes, resilience comes more easily for some people than for others. But it's not finite. It's not limited by availability to a select few. It's yours to possess and claim once you acknowledge where your level of resilience is in your set of coping skills. Your family legacy, the situations that you've dealt with, the outcome of those situations, as well as your emotional wiring tendencies for drama or calm are filters in resilience like they are in all the other factors that shape you. That's why we started there in this book before we got to the solving part of a problem. It's also the reason effective problem solving is multifaceted. It's not complicated, but it has lots of components. Insight into those filters that affect the lens of your worldview will help you discover ways to increase your tolerance for difficulty. Remember, they are the cornerstone of your foundation. They are the *Start Here* place on your roadmap. It's like cracking the code.

In the middle of any problem you're seeking relief. Through that process you gain resilience. It's the by-product of survival. You know deep in your survivalist gut that you'll find a way through, even if you can't fathom that in this moment. It's that innate will to live. That's as much a part of your DNA as eye color. What you want is that feeling of strength. That something within that says you can do this, even when your doubting, exhausted mind and your weary heart say you can't. You need that unshakeable confidence to support you as you cope through to the other side of the difficulty. Where do you find it? How do you get it?

I'm always amazed at how difficult we can make things. I see books on how to be more resilient. There are experts weighing in on finding it. Well my friend, I'm here to let you in on something. Here's your Glinda the Good Witch moment. I look pretty good in a tiara, wave a wand well, and love a ball gown, so guess who's your Glinda? Listen to me closely.

Resilience is your pair of sparkly ruby slippers.

You have the power within you already and it grows every time you face difficulty.

Your experiences build resilience. Failures and disappointments are like weights to lift. Once you make the effort to take them on and move them out of your way, you get an added bonus. Repeated resistance builds muscle. You build resilience as you bear more weight each time a difficulty arises. Each problem is an added weight. Then an emotional memory muscle develops that will serve you every time you call upon it. Think of it as building bulk. It will make the lifting easier and more effortless as you go.

Let's talk about it using architectural terms again. You are adding insulation to protect the interior of your structure from the outside elements; the cold, the heat, the wind, and the rain. You're reinforcing the very bones upon which it's built.

That organic process of resilience will evolve as you live your life. Every experience that brings any disappointment, hurt, or dissatisfaction makes a deposit in your resilience account. Each negative will leave you with a gift of some size in the form of wisdom, savvy, and resilience. Let's talk about that.

- Do you think you're resilient?

- What problems have you experienced that have contributed to your resilience account?

- Looking back on past situations, haven't you seen the blessing in the disappointment? Otherwise, you wouldn't have been in the right place at the right time for the great thing that happened next.

- Haven't you said after time passed and events revealed much, that someone did you a favor when they rejected you? Rejection is often God's protection.

- Has a past problem opened you to resources that you might not have discovered? Often a resource you find when dealing with a problem comes into play to your advantage in a future situation, mitigating it in a way that wouldn't have happened without that knowledge.

- Do you see that resilience is a quantifiable resource?

You can also intentionally call resilience in and claim it consciously.

When something presents in your life as a problem, stop and think of all the times you've managed difficulty in the past. The walls were caving in, but you survived. Reflect on the reality that you've made it through before and know that you will again. These are the stones that you put in place to build a retaining wall to prop you up and stop the slow erosion of disappointment. Remember the things you thought at the time were problems that turned out to be blessings in disguise. I know that might be hard right now, but you have those in your coping kit for a reason. They are tools with your name on them.

This is positivity at its strongest and most measurable. Make it tangible in your mind. Stand on the adversity you've experienced to gain a better vantage point to see the road up ahead. Use it to look past the present pain or discomfort and visualize a better future beyond.

Take it further. Give your resilience a shape in your mind. Be creative.

See it as whatever says "protection" to you.

A shield.

A lightsaber.

A moat around your castle.

A big badass dog.

Resilience is that barrier between you and the negatives of the world. Isn't that what you need right now? Wouldn't that be a huge relief? Think of it as your shark cage. The problem is circling, it may have its menacing jaws flung wide open, but it can't penetrate the steel protecting you.

Think of resilience as good resistance.

There's that word meaning thing again. Turn the word usage to your advantage. Resistance is most often used to mean to struggle against or to oppose. Let's use it that way but for good. Use your resilience in opposition to depression. Wield it as a weapon against disappointment. Resist the anger, the resentment, the self-pity, the heartache.

Victory by victory, success by success, apply the skills you're developing and honing. Bind them together to make a force field of resilience around you.

You've done so much to move yourself forward through this difficult problem by exploring this information and considering these strategies. You have the extra bonus with this insight of developing empathy for others who are in distress. The kind of empathy that is trial-tested. You know where they are because you've been there yourself. Any chance you have to help someone else with this genuine empathy, you reinforce your resilience.

I have fabulous news.

There's more reward from your willingness to find a workable solution to the problem in your life. Implementing and practicing these strategies has a lasting effect that goes way beyond the situation you're in now. It may have inhibited you, held you back, or even stopped you, but you can move it with a commitment to positive action. Then you get to see it serve you, not only in this moment, but again and again as many times as you call upon it.

It will not fail you.

It will not leave you.

It will build your confidence with the knowledge that you ARE resilient.

CHAPTER FOURTEEN:

ASK FOR HELP

Sometimes obtaining and maintaining emotional equilibrium takes more than personal development strategies. While I humbly offer you those common-sense strategies, they are not intended to be a substitute for professional assessment and physician supervision. *Mental wellness* is the part of taking care of your emotional and mental health that can be accomplished by your efforts. *Mental illness* requires professional care. Sometimes a problem is bigger than any best effort you can muster against it. The black hole can be too deep and the climb out too steep. You find yourself in need of more. Knowing you need assistance when you have exhausted your own resources is one of the best coping strategies you can use.

There are some questions to ask yourself to determine if you are a candidate for professional help.

- Is the problem you are facing interfering with your functioning?

- Have you experienced a loss of interest in your personal relationships?

- Are you aware of any personality changes in yourself that are unfavorable?

- Are you experiencing sleep disruption that is affecting your ability to work or interact with others in a productive way?

- Are you relying on alcohol or drugs to cope?

- Do you have a lingering feeling of hopelessness?

- Have you had any thoughts of harming yourself or others?

If your mental wellness is at risk beyond the strategies you've learned, then you owe it to yourself and the ones you love to seek help. Don't let denial defeat you. Use it to work for you and move you forward by denying stress access to your spirit.

Asking for help is an act of bravery.
It is also an act of love.

We all can truly break down and banish the stigma of mental health and its treatment beginning with our willingness to recognize that anyone can need help, and everyone deserves to have it available to them. To that end, everyone benefits.

There is a wide range of professional help available. Physician supervised treatment and intervention for assessment, medication management, therapy, support groups, and rehabilitation must be considered as necessary and blessed resources. Thank God for the dedicated and gifted nurse practitioners, physicians, therapists, and counselors (and all the tools they possess) to shepherd you through to healing. Sometimes a combination of modalities may be needed for the best result. Let those who are trained, equipped, and willing be of service to you.

There are many resources available in your community. Your primary physician is a great start. School counselors are a wonderful resource for children and teens. There are online resources as well.

If you believe you need professional help, reaching out is your best next step in Coping Smart.

CHAPTER FIFTEEN:

AGAIN, SO YOU'LL KNOW

I began this book telling you a little bit about my story so you could trust that I personally know what it's like to be in the middle of a difficulty. I gave you a synopsis of my abbreviated childhood and those challenges. Then I sketched an outline of the second crisis later in mid-life. These times were the foundation of the strategies that I developed for my survival and then what I came to call my *thrival*. Isn't that the ultimate and optimum goal of finding the way out of trouble: to thrive despite the odds?

So that you'll grasp the idea that the scope of possible human problems is wide and the call to cope is ever present, I'll share with you the impetus for the existence of this book. I think you will relate in many ways, and hopefully you'll see that no one is immune from problems throughout their life. The sooner you come to that acceptance, the easier it will be to cope. Remember that knowledge is power.

As I mentioned earlier, I have had several iterations of my life over the years. I have continued to counsel people on a one-on-one basis but on a limited scale as life has given me other road signs to follow and my family's needs have changed.

Before the pandemic shook the globe in 2020, my career shifted to include a new purpose as daytime caregiver for my three grand-children while their parents pursued their careers. I was "on duty," as I lovingly described my chosen vocation, from 7:00 a.m. to 7:00 p.m.

five days a week and available on the weekends for shuttle service or babysitting for the youngest while the older two participated in their extracurricular activities. My second time at the rodeo was unbelievably fun and exhausting and beyond the biggest blessing. I was fortunate to be in great health and young enough to really enjoy getting to be such a viable part of their everyday life.

You know what happened next. It happened to all of us in varying degrees.

Remote learning for my grandkids and stay-at-home orders for their parents was a blessing in the chaos that allowed them to spend so much time together. Thankfully they adapted to the new normal and became shining examples of resilience. I couldn't have been more pleased or prouder of all of them. But like the rest of the planet, a sadness of being physically separated seeped deep into my being.

Overnight, I found myself from being in the center of their everyday lives to having no daily contact with my sun and my moon and my stars (my grandchildren), a business on hold, no idea when either would return, and no familiar bearings on the road of my life. I had a husband whose work required traveling over a hundred thousand miles a year suddenly at a standstill, his mind unable to wrap around the idea that what he had done his entire life had stopped. My business partner and I considered ways to pivot and survive until a vaccine could open us again. My medical professional child was in the chaos of an overwhelmed mental health care system guiding her patients through the uncertainty. My other professional child was handling two full-time jobs seven days a week from a home office in the dining room while she managed three kids at home. They gave up what should have been all the normal childhood events with brave tenacity. There was much to be worried about and the anxiety threatened.

I also scrolled the news and saw the statistics of rising depression and suicide rates. I watched talk-show television and heard the despair in people's voices and recognized that fear in their eyes. My passion for helping hurting people stirred as I acknowledged the growing negativity as the positivity blasts came and went and the problems remained.

Like you, at first I cleaned out closets and organized drawers. Next, I began binge-watching all the shows I had been too busy being busy to follow. Then, I fought off the fear that came with the news every day and the paralysis of the unknown while I foraged for toilet paper. I used the Seven R's I had developed early on and knew so well to cope and keep calm. It worked for the mounting stress. As the weeks crawled by and the reality sunk in that my financial situation had no remedy in sight, I realized I was standing in the black hole again. It was soul-numbing to think I was facing starting over yet again. Then my problem-solving muscle kicked in. I sat down and started formulating my survival plan. I was in a full-blown crisis, and I knew what I had to do. It was time to identify the problems and the emotional toll, clarify my options and a plan, and manage the stress until a workable solution presented.

Something miraculous happened that gave me direction. People I hadn't heard from in years reached out to me for my advice because they remembered and believed in my methodology for problem solving and stress management and trusted it. They needed a path out of the stress that was stealing their sleep, their peace, and their joy. They were happy for the newfound time with their families and at the same time they were struggling with anxiety and depression. Some had specific problems like trying to stay positive when they couldn't pay their mortgage, or how to care for their kids when they were being asked to go back into the office, or where to get a job when their employer shuttered. Most were unsettled by the uncertainty. Some were aggravated that life had somehow turned on them despite their best efforts. Many had a feeling they couldn't name and couldn't shake that was weighing them down.

As I heard myself recounting the proven strategies and helping them see through the fog of confusion we've talked about in this book together, it became clear what I needed to do next. I felt passionately that what I knew should be shared with so many others struggling with the overwhelming stress. It was time to return fulltime and get back on the road where I saw so many stalled and in need of assistance.

My purpose was calling again.

My answer was Coping Smart.

I believe with every fiber of my being that it can be yours as well.

I tell you this because I am an example of what you are looking for in this tough moment. I've been face down but refused to go belly up. I've been stuck in emotional quicksand but resisted the pull. I've heard the returned echo of my pleas for help from the bottom of the black hole but ascended up and out with prayer. I have reinvented, reinstated, reinvigorated, restarted, reiterated, reset, replenished, restored, and received relief. I state this not from a viewpoint of my saying, 'look at me and all the bad things I have had to endure,' but because I want you to look at my story and see yourself.

You know that you have something inside you that believes in second chances. In this moment, you probably think those only happen for others. I want you to believe yours is coming. I also want you to understand and allow that understanding to seep into your bones that there is no limit to the number of second chances or the times you can ask.

I want you to have the peace that comes with accepting you can move the problem you're facing. I want you to know that prayer is the major coping skill for clarity and hope. That belief in yourself is a prayer all its own and the greatest of affirmations. Prayers do get answered and if you don't get what you ask for, you'll get what you need. You'll know, even if it takes time before you know, it was better than what you asked for.

Celebrate this moment. You are back on the road and headed forward. Lean into these strategies to morph the anxiety that threatens your peace into joyful expectation. Use the skills you've discovered here as sparks and build your fire. Warm yourself with the love in which they are offered. Dance in the glow of their certainty. Know that I am on the side of your road cheering you on when you find yourself pulling one foot slowly behind the other. I'm reaching for you when you stumble. I'm willing you to uprightness and shouting Halleujah when you streak past on your way to the place you define as happiness and success.

You honor me with the privilege.

Acknowledgements

Writing is the most solitary endeavor requiring the multiple efforts of many.

To the craftsmen, Daniel Reiff my website wizard, Ben Groner my copy editor, Clark Kenyon the master formatter, Monica Van Landingham the social media mama, Judith Hill my magical photographer and Kenzi Galloway my fabulous stylist for my author photos I thank you all.

To Jeremy Glisson my graphics designer extraordinaire, your talent is matched only by your patience and kindness. Thank you for supporting me through this process.

I owe so much to my writer tribe beginning with J. Suzanne Frank, Barbara Miercort, and the late great Bob Banner at The SMU Writer's Path, and The Sewanee Writers' Conference students and faculty, and The Maui Writers' Workshop.

To my steadfast Dallas writers group all-star members Christine, Kirsten, Alecia, Renee, Margaret, and Amy as well as the incomparable and much-missed Betty who was my on the road workshop buddy.

Special thanks to Margaret Patterson for her keen eye for authenticity and wicked sense of humor.

Much love and thanks to Ann Patchett and Sparky for the early morning walks and talks that were my saving grace slice of normality in the pandemic shutdown. And to my Henry who walks me.

I humbly thank the talented Joanne Gordan who gave this book its structure with her editorial expertise and gave me direction, courage, and moral support.

My love of writing was inspired by my teacher Beth Clay whose encouragement to my teenage self sparked my writer's fire. She showed me words have the power to transform.

I give much thanks and love to my mother Nancy who always said yes when I needed her to. My love of books was imprinted early on by her reverence for their power to transport.

To the fabulous and patient Patsy Bailey Queen of Social Media and best cheerleader I could ever ask for, I am forever grateful.

To Leah I am so grateful for your unwavering faith and support for this and everything I do. I am so very proud of all you have accomplished. To Lauren I thank you for my three girls and for being the great role model you are for them and for bringing Greg into our lives.

Much gratitude goes to Buster Corley head of my Advisory Board for being my mentor, wise counsel, and for his support of this endeavor.

To Richard my greatest champion and number one fan, I owe more appreciation than could possibly be given in more ways than could possibly be counted for more reasons that could possibly be expressed. Love tells our story every day.

About the Author

Becki Pickett has spent a life time devoted to understanding human behavior and relationships. Her life experiences, successes and challenges have equipped her with an intuitive empathy for others. Her opportunities as wife, mother, grandmother, entrepreneur, business owner, grief support facilitator, personal development and emotional wellness expert, speaker, author, advocate of intentional parenting, and champion of the human spirit have provided her with a unique insight into the nuances of problem and stress management. She currently lives in Nashville with her husband Richard and her sweet dog Henry.

Becki is available to speak to groups of all sizes for all manner of problem management. Whether one-on-one or an auditorium capacity crowd, Becki brings an authentic desire to use her experience and knowledge to serve.

Please visit: copingsmart.com or email: becki@copingsmart.com

More Coping Smart.

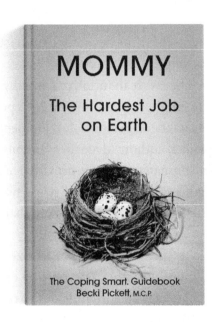

The Ultimate Mom Manual

Workable wisdom for every age, stage,
and phase along the way.

Coming in Summer 2021. To learn more visit www.copingsmart.com

Made in the USA
Monee, IL
02 August 2021